MUSLIM BELIEFS AND ISSUES

Michael Keene

CONTENTS

Unit

1	What is Islam?	4
2	Who are the Muslims?	6
3	Sunni and Shi'ite Muslims	8
4	Allah	10
5	The Five Pillars of Islam	12
6	The Shahadah	14
7	Salah	16
8	Du'a	18
9	The Hajj	20
10	The Day of Judgement	22
11	The Ummah	24
12	The Qur'an	26
13	Using the Qur'an	28
14	The Sunnah	30
15	Family life	32
16	Childhood	34
17	Marriage	36
18	Dealing with death	38
19	The place of women in Islam	40
20	Old age	42
21	Living as a Muslim	44
22	Sawm	46
23	The mosque	48
24	Inside a mosque	50
25	Muslims in Britain	52
26	The 'haves' and the 'have-nots'	54
27	Zakah and sadaqah	56
28	Islamic Relief Worldwide	58
29	Creation and Paradise	60
30	Stewards of creation	62
31	The Muslim attitude to animals	64
32	The Jihad	66
33	Islam and science	68
	Glossary	70

WHAT IS ISLAM?

You will find out

- The link between Islam, Judaism and Christianity.
- About the Prophet Muhammad.
- About Islam in the world today.
- What it means to be a Muslim.

In the glossary

Abraham

Allah

Five Pillars

Makkah

Mosque

Muhammad

Prophet

Qur'an

Shahadah

Ummah

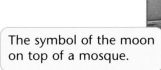

The symbol of the moon on top of a mosque.

Islam is one of the most important religions in the world. It is a sister religion to Judaism and Christianity since all three religions have a spiritual link with the **prophet** Ibrahim [**Abraham**]. Muslims regard themselves, along with Christians and Jews, as 'people of the Book'. This means that they believe that the revelation of God has reached them through a whole line of prophets – including Ibrahim, Nuh [Noah], Musa [Moses], Isa [Jesus] and **Muhammad**.

THE PROPHET MUHAMMAD

Islam teaches that there have been many prophets in history from Noah onwards. The last and greatest of the prophets, however, was Muhammad. The whole religion of Islam is based on the revelations that were given by **Allah** [God] to the Prophet Muhammad. These revelations form the content of the **Qur'an**, the holy book of Islam.

Muhammad was born in 570CE in the city of **Makkah** in Arabia. From Arabia, the religion of Islam flowed rapidly and strongly throughout the world. Its natural home, however, has always been the Middle East.

ISLAM IN TODAY'S WORLD

Today, Islam is a worldwide religion and is followed by about 25% of the world's population [1,800 billion people]. Countries in the Middle East and North Africa such as Saudi Arabia, Egypt, Iraq, Tunisia and Libya are almost exclusively Muslim. So, too, are many countries in Central Asia. The majority of the population in Pakistan, Bangladesh and Indonesia are also Muslim. There are around two million Muslims in Britain and you will find out more about them in unit 25.

TAKE TIME TO THINK

The religions of Islam, Christianity and Judaism have a great deal in common with each other. Describe two things that you have already discovered that the three religions share with each other.

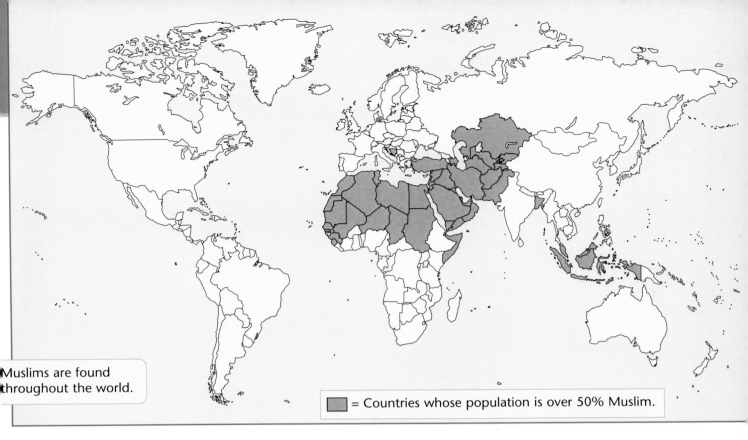

Muslims are found throughout the world.

⬛ = Countries whose population is over 50% Muslim.

ISLAM AND MUSLIMS

Wherever Muslims are found they are united in their faith. They belong to a worldwide community of believers which is called the **Ummah**. There is more about the Ummah in unit 11.

It is important to remember that:

- All Muslims believe that there is one God [Allah] and that Muhammad is His messenger. This statement of faith is known as the **Shahadah** and is the basic belief of all Muslims. You will find out more about the Shahadah, the first of the **Five Pillars** of Islam, in unit 6.

- The word 'Islam' can have more than one meaning. It can mean:
  - 'submission to God' – a Muslim submits himself or herself to the will of Allah as this is made known in the Qur'an.
  - 'peace' – the Prophet Muhammad said that a good Muslim is someone who always brings Allah's peace with them.

Islam is an inner struggle to rise above the so-called attractions of this life and to show true dedication to Allah. This dedication requires regular prayer and a true Muslim must also do their best for their family, orphans, the needy and the sick.

OVER TO **YOU** ▶▶▶

1 Why do Muslims regard Christianity and Judaism as sister religions to Islam?

2 What is a prophet?

3 Write two sentences about:
   a) Muhammad
   b) Allah
   c) The Qur'an

4 Look at the map in this spread. Using an atlas to help you, make a list of ten countries in the world where more than 50% of the population is Muslim.

5 You can see the symbol of Islam – the crescent moon – on page 4. It is found on the top of every **mosque**, a Muslim place of worship.
   a) Copy the symbol into your book.
   b) Why do you think that this is an appropriate symbol for Islam?

   Clue: Early Muslims largely lived in desert areas and they made use of the moon – but how?

WHO ARE THE MUSLIMS?

You will find out

- The four basic beliefs of all Muslims.

- The distinctive way of life that every Muslim is expected to follow.

In the glossary

Allah

Angel Jibril

Muhammad

Prophet

Qur'an

By prostrating themselves during their prayers, these Muslims are submitting themselves to the will of Allah.

Muslims throughout the world are distinguished by:

1 THEIR BELIEFS

Here are four of the most important, and distinctive, beliefs to which all Muslims are committed. Each is explained at later stages in the book:

Belief 1 There is only one God – Allah – who has created all things. Allah guides all those who submit themselves to Him in the right path. We will find out much more about Allah in unit 4.

Belief 2 Muhammad was the last, and the greatest, of the many prophets sent into the world by Allah. Muhammad received the final and complete revelation of Allah's truth from the **Angel Jibril** in a series of revelations which are contained in the Qur'an. The work of every prophet, and of Muhammad, was to preach Allah's Word to the people in the hope that they would change their ways and believe the truth.

Belief 3 The Qur'an, the holy book of Islam, contains the final message of Allah to humankind, as revealed to Muhammad. It contains moral and spiritual guidance for all Muslims. You will find out more about the Qur'an and the way in which it is used by Muslims in units 12 and 13.

Belief 4 The Qur'an refers to the Day of Judgement when Allah will judge every man and woman according to the deeds they have committed. It urges people to live righteous and upright lives and always to seek to do good to other people. You can find out more about the Muslim belief in life after death in unit 10.

2 A WAY OF LIFE

Allah has not left his followers without any guidance to help them through life. The Qur'an encourages them to reflect on their actions and to seek the will of Allah at all times. It places on each Muslim the duty to:

CHECK IT OUT

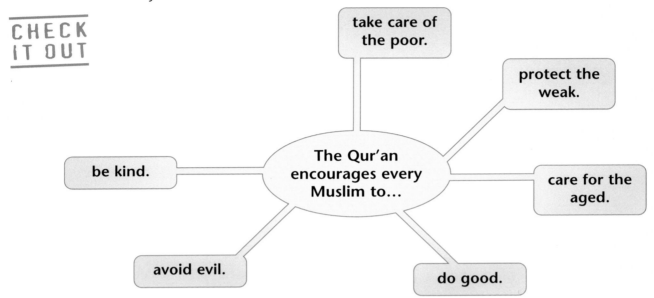

Muslim history reveals many examples of people who have set a high moral standard for themselves and encouraged others to do the same. They will have been inspired in their everyday lives by:

- The example of the Prophet Muhammad.
- The sacrifices made by the family of the Prophet.
- The struggle of the early Muslims to fight injustice and oppression.

These are the examples that every Muslim seeks to follow.

TAKE TIME TO THINK

What do you think is the relationship between Muhammad and the other prophets, including Moses and Jesus, that Allah sent into the world?

OVER TO YOU ▶▶▶

1 Copy and complete each of the following sentences from the phrases listed below:
   a) Muslims believe in one God – …
   b) There were many prophets but the last was…
   c) Muhammad received a series of … from Allah.
   d) The role of every prophet was to …
   e) On the … every person will have to face Allah and account for their deeds.

> Day of Judgement – Allah – Revelations – Preach Allah's Word – Muhammad

2 What is the Day of Judgement?
3 What distinctive way of life are Muslims expected to follow?

SUNNI AND SHI'ITE MUSLIMS

You will find out

- About Sunni Muslims.
- About Shi'ite Muslims.

In the glossary

Allah

Hadith

Imam

Muhammad

Prophet

Qur'an

Shahadah

Shi'ite Muslims

Sunnah

Sunni Muslims

Ulama

When the Prophet Muhammad was alive, Muslims would go to him when they had a question to ask or a dispute to settle among themselves. When he died, however, his followers could not agree on a leader to succeed him. This disagreement led to a division in the Muslim community. Islam divided into two branches – known as Sunni and Shi'ite:

1 THE SUNNI MUSLIMS

Some Muslims believed that the Prophet had not appointed anyone to succeed him. These Muslims became known as Sunnis – 'people who follow the **Sunnah** of the Prophet' – his example in what he said and did. The Sunnis believed that all that Muslims need to live the life that Allah expects of them are:

- The Qur'an
- The Sunnah [You will find out more about this in unit 14.]
- The example of the Prophet Muhammad.

The Sunnis relied on learned members of the community to produce rules of conduct by studying the Qur'an and the **Hadith**. They used their judgement, local customs and agreement among themselves to produce the rules.

The Sunnis agreed that the Muslim community must have a leader. He was known as the caliph and was elected by important members of the community [the **ulama**]. His main task was to maintain law and order so that people could follow their religion and live their lives in peace. The first caliph was Abu Bakr, the much respected companion of the Prophet.

Sunnis are by far the largest branch of Islam. 9 out of every 10 Muslims belong to the Sunni branch.

2 THE SHI'ITE MUSLIMS

Other Muslims believed that Muhammad had already named his successor. He was Ali, the Prophet's cousin and son-in-law, who was married to Fatima, Muhammad's daughter. These people believed that Muhammad had said that his followers should not only follow the teachings of the Qur'an but also a leader chosen from the Prophet's own family.

Ali was the first leader, or **imam**, of the Shi'ites. They supported Ali's claim that the leadership of the Muslims belonged to him. The Shi'ites believe in a line of leaders from the Prophet and Ali. They believe that:

- The Sunnah of the Prophet should be closely followed.
- The traditions of the imams are extremely important.
- Although Ali claimed that he was the imam, he co-operated with Abu Bakr and the two caliphs after him. He also praised the conduct of Abu Bakr and the second caliph, Umar, for what they had done for Islam. Sunni Muslims also respect Ali as the fourth caliph.

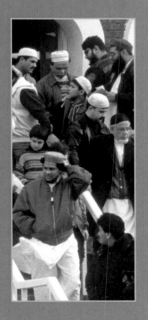

1 How did the early Muslims depend on the Prophet Muhammad and what happened after he died?
2 What did the early Muslims disagree about that led to the split between Sunni and Shi'ite Muslims?
3 Write down ten pieces of information about the Sunni Muslims.
4 Write down ten pieces of information about the Shi'ite Muslims.
5 Describe two differences between Sunni and Shi'ite Muslims.

TWO GROUPS – ONE FAITH

CHECK
IT OUT

agree on the importance of the Shahadah.

believe that all Muslims should act with peace and responsibility.

Both Sunni and Shi'ite Muslims...

follow the Sunnah of Muhammad.

believe that Muhammad is the greatest of Allah's prophets.

Most Muslims believe that, though there are deep differences between Sunnis and Shi'ites, they do belong to the one faith.

You will find out

- The different names of Allah.
- The oneness of Allah.
- The dependency of human beings on Allah.

In the glossary

Allah

Hadith

Mosque

Muhammad

Prophet

Qur'an

Tasbih

Tawhid

There is one belief in Islam that is more important than any other – that there is only one God, Allah, and that Muhammad is His messenger. The name Allah means 'the God'. Allah has spoken to the world through His prophets and the last, and greatest, of these was Muhammad.

THE NAMES OF ALLAH

The Qur'an asks believers to remember Allah through His Beautiful Names. According to the Hadith of the Prophet Muhammad, there are 99 such names. Here are ten of Allah's Beautiful Names:

CHECK IT OUT

In the Qur'an, Allah is...

- The Everlasting
- The All-High
- The Knower of the Unseen
- The All-Seeing
- The King
- The Eternal
- The All-Holy
- The All-Knowing
- The All-Mighty
- The Compassionate

A Muslim is able to call on any of these names, night or day. In the words of the Qur'an:

A *"The most beautiful names belong to God, so call on Him by them."*

These names are repeated continually throughout the day. To help a Muslim there are special beads called **tasbih** which can be used.

TAKE TIME TO THINK

Muslims believe that it is very important that they put Allah first in their lives. What is the first, and the most important, thing in your life? Why is it so important to you?

NONE TO BE WORSHIPPED BUT ALLAH,MUHAMMED PEACE BE UPON HIM IS HIS MESSENGER

Muslims worshipping in this mosque are reminded about their priorities.

This man is remembering the different Names of Allah.

ALLAH IS ONE

Muslims believe that Allah is One. This belief is called the **Tawhid**. This means that Allah is beyond all human understanding. He cannot be compared to anyone or anything else. He is unique. He knows everything, sees everything and can do anything. The Qur'an says:

> B *"No mortal [human] eyes can see Him, though He sees all eyes, He is the All-Subtle, the All-Aware."*
>
> Qur'an. Surah 6.103

Allah is the creator of everything that exists. Nothing can exist unless Allah has made it. Because He has made all things, He is also the Judge of everyone. He is all-powerful. Yet Allah is full of mercy to everyone who submits to Him.

ALLAH AND THE WORLD

All men and women depend entirely on Allah. They owe their beginning in the womb to Him. They continue to exist because of His mercy. They only draw breath because Allah allows it. The moment that permission is withdrawn, the person dies. This is why everyone owes it to Allah to submit to Him.

OVER TO **YOU** ▶▶▶

1 What is the most important belief in Islam?

2 There is a beautiful Muslim legend which explains why Allah has 99 and not 100 Names. According to the legend, there is one more Name for Allah but this is only known to the camel. Behind this legend there is an important spiritual truth. What do you think it is?

3 Among other Names, Allah is called the Compassionate, the Merciful, the Forgiver and the Wise.

   a) Find out some of the other Names of Allah.

   b) Are there any Names on the list that surprise you? If so, try to explain why.

   c) Make a list of the names given to God in one other religion that you know about. Are any of these names similar to those given to Allah by Muslims?

4 What is the Tawhid?

THE FIVE PILLARS OF ISLAM

You will find out

- About the Shahadah.
- About salah.
- About sawm.
- About zakah.
- About the Hajj.

In the glossary

Allah

Five Pillars

Hajj

Makkah

Mosque

Muhammad

Prophet

Qur'an

Ramadan

Salah

Sawm

Shahadah

Zakah

Muslims believe that all human beings have been created by Allah and so nothing can happen to them by chance or accident. Those human beings who appear to be the least important in human eyes – the poor, the needy, the orphans and the widows – are actually the most important to Allah.

The Qur'an often tells people to believe in Allah and do good. In Islam, a belief in Allah and doing good go together. To help people to live pleasing lives to Allah, they have been given His guidance. This comes in the form of five Pillars on which each person is encouraged to build their everyday lives [A].

A *"Islam is founded on five pillars: faith; regular prayer; almsgiving; fasting in Ramadan and going on pilgrimage."*

Muhammad

PILLAR 1: THE SHAHADAH – FAITH IN ALLAH

This is the Pillar on which the whole faith of Islam is based. The Shahadah is a statement of faith that contains two of the most important beliefs in Islam:

- That there is only one God.
- That Muhammad is the greatest of Allah's prophets.

Most Muslims repeat the Shahadah several times a day. You will find out about the Shahadah in unit 6.

B *"I witness that there is no God but Allah and that Muhammad is the Messenger of Allah."*

PILLAR 2: SALAH – PRAYER

Muslims are expected to keep Allah in the forefront of their thoughts all day. To help them to do this they are expected to pray five times each day – at set times. They can do this in the mosque, in their home, in their workplace or in the open-air. You will find out more about **salah** in unit 7.

PILLAR 3: SAWM – FASTING

Muslims fast, go without food or water, during daylight hours during the month of **Ramadan**. This has two purposes:

- It gives Muslims the opportunity of spending more time than usual thinking about Allah, reading the Qur'an and praying.
- It helps Muslims to remember members of their community who do not have the basic necessities of life.

You will find out more about **sawm** in unit 22.

After the Shahadah, prayer is the most important of the Five Pillars of Islam.

PILLAR 4: ZAKAH – ALMSGIVING

Zakah is almsgiving. Muslims are expected to give at least 2.5% of their savings to help the poor every year. Muslims believe that all wealth comes from Allah and so belongs to Him. In sharing their wealth with those who are less fortunate, they are only doing what Allah expects of them. You will find out more about zakah in unit 27.

PILLAR 5: HAJJ – PILGRIMAGE

The final Pillar of Islam is the pilgrimage to the holy city of Makkah. Every Muslim is expected to undertake this once during their lifetime. The **Hajj** is all about drawing as close as possible to Allah and each other by visiting places that are holy to all Muslims. You can find out more about the Hajj in unit 9.

TAKE TIME TO THINK

Muslims believe that setting aside regular times for prayer gives their life a structure. What is it that gives your life a structure? Do you think that it is important for everyone to have some kind of structure in their life? Why?

OVER TO YOU ▶▶▶

1 What is the Shahadah?
2 Why do you think that Muslims base their lives on a statement of belief?
3 Many religions believe that fasting is important. What do you think that a person might get from going without food and drink for a short time?
4 The holy city of Makkah is very important to all Muslims. Is there a place that is 'holy' or very important to you? Try to explain why.

THE SHAHADAH

You will find out

- Why the Shahadah is important to Muslims.
- The call of the mu'adhin.

In the glossary

Adhan

Allah

Five Pillars

Mosque

Mu'adhin

Muhammad

Prophet

Qur'an

Shahadah

Shi'ite Muslims

Sunni Muslims

Tawhid

The Shahadah is the first, and the most important, of the Five Pillars of Islam.

THE SHAHADAH

In unit 5, you found out about the Five Pillars of Islam. The first, and the most important, of the Pillars is a statement of faith in Allah and in Muhammad, Allah's Prophet. This is called the Shahadah and you can find it in Extract A:

A *"There is no God but Allah, Muhammad is the messenger of Allah."*

'Shahadah' is the Aramaic word meaning 'witness'. In saying the Shahadah, Muslims are bearing witness to their faith in Allah and Islam. This statement of faith is so important to Muslims that they repeat it every day. It contains two key statements:

- Muslims believe that Allah is the One and Only God. This belief is called Tawhid – a word which means 'unity'. It means that Allah is beyond all human understanding and cannot be compared to anything else. He is unique. He knows everything, sees everything and can do anything. You can see what the Qur'an has to say about this in Extract B:

B *"Such is God, your Lord. There is no God but Him, the Creator of all things. Therefore serve Him. Of all things He is the Guardian."*

Qur'an. Surah 6.2

- Allah has spoken to humankind and revealed knowledge about Himself. He has done this through the greatest of his prophets – Muhammad. The message that Allah gave to Muhammad is recorded in the words of the Qur'an. This is Allah's holy book. It contains the actual 'Words of Allah' which have been faithfully recorded in its pages.

In Britain, the mu'adhin issues the call to prayer from inside the mosque. Muslims are expected to respond to it wherever they are and whatever they are doing.

THE IMPORTANCE OF THE SHAHADAH

When a person can say the Shahadah, and mean it totally in their hearts, they are a true Muslim. A Muslim will say the Shahadah thousands of times in their lifetime. In particular, they will:

- repeat it many times each day between getting up in the morning and going to bed at night.
- whisper it into the ear of every newborn baby.
- teach it to their children as soon as they are old enough to learn it.
- hope that it will be the last words to cross their lips before they die.

OVER TO YOU ▶▶▶

1 How do we know that the Shahadah is extremely important to all Muslims?
2 Copy the words of the call to prayer into your book. Write down three things that we learn from it about Muslim belief.

THE CALL OF THE MU'ADHIN

Muhammad arrived in the city of Madinah in 622CE. One of his earliest companions was Bilal, a converted Abyssinian slave. Muhammad told him to call the faithful to prayer five times a day and Bilal used the words of the Shahadah to do so. These words still form part of the call to prayer [the **Adhan**] that the mu'adhin delivers five times daily. The full Sunni call to prayer is found in Extract C:

C *"God is great [four times]*
I bear witness that there is no god but Allah [twice]
I bear witness that Muhammad is the Prophet of God [twice]
Come to prayer! [twice]
Come to success! [twice]
God is great! [twice]
There is no god but God"

[Shi'ites add "Come to perform the best of deeds" twice after the fifth line]

You will find out

- How a Muslim prepares for prayer [salah].
- The importance and meaning of wudu.
- The meaning of salah for every Muslim.

In the glossary

Allah

Madinah

Makkah

Mosque

Muhammad

Prophet

Qur'an

Rak'ah

Salah

Wudu

Muslims do not find it easy to live in this world as witnesses to Allah as many other things demand their attention. If they wish to be committed to Allah, some discipline is needed. Muslims are encouraged to pray [salah] five times a day to direct their thoughts away from the pressures of this life to Allah.

PREPARATION FOR SALAH

Salah begins with washing and this is called **wudu**. There are special washing facilities in the courtyards of most mosques. Wudu always follows the same procedure once a worshipper has announced their intention of praying to Allah.

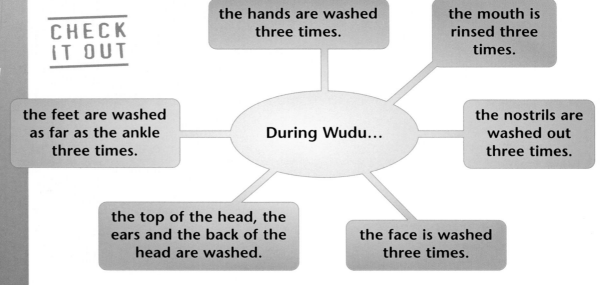

CHECK IT OUT

During Wudu...

- the hands are washed three times.
- the mouth is rinsed three times.
- the nostrils are washed out three times.
- the face is washed three times.
- the top of the head, the ears and the back of the head are washed.
- the feet are washed as far as the ankle three times.

SALAH

Prayer does not have to take place in a mosque. It can be carried out in any public place as long as:

- The person is clean. If no running water is available then clean sand will do for wudu.
- The place is clean. Muslims use a prayer mat to make sure of this. All prayer mats have an arch on them which is pointed towards Makkah.

A   *'If one of you has a river at his door in which he washes himself five times a day, what do you think? Would it leave any dirt on him?' The companions said, 'It will not leave any dirt on him.' The Prophet said, 'This is an example of the five prayers with which Allah blots out the evils of man.'*

Hadith

To perform salah, Muslims follow a sequence of movements and accompany them with quotations from the Qur'an. The movements involve standing, bowing or kneeling face down on the floor. Each cycle of movements is called a **rak'ah**. Rak'ahs must be done at each of the times set aside for prayer. The exact number performed varies from two to four depending on the time of day.

WHAT IS PRAYER ABOUT?

It is important to remember that prayer for each Muslim is about:

1 Remembering that Allah is central to everything that happens to a believer. An essential part of prayer is thanking Allah for the blessings of everyday life.
2 Realising that every Muslim has heavy responsibilities towards Allah. A Muslim works them out through prayer and reading the Qur'an.
3 Through wudu, a Muslim realises that their whole body is involved in worshipping Allah – it is a physical as well as a spiritual duty.
4 Prayer interrupts the daily round of life and reminds the Muslim that Allah makes the first demand on everyone. Prayer is time set aside for Allah alone.

Salah, however, is not the whole of prayer – it is a bare minimum. There is always an opportunity for Muslims to pray if there is something they particularly need to pray about at any time [unit 8].

B "*The prayer said in Madinah is worth thousands of others, except that in Makkah, which is worth a hundred thousand. But worth more than all this is the prayer said in the house where no-one sees but God and which has no other object than to draw close to God.*"

Hadith

Almost at the end of prayer, a Muslim prostrates himself or herself. This shows that they totally accept the authority of Allah.

OVER TO **YOU** ▶▶▶

1 More than once the Prophet Muhammad likened prayer to washing one's body in a stream. What do you think he meant by this?
2 Read the quotation from Muhammad in Extract B. Find out why Makkah and Madinah are mentioned as the two places where praying is so valuable.

TAKE TIME TO THINK

The washing of the body before salah is very elaborate and can take several minutes. Why do you think that the Qur'an insists on running water being used?

DU'A

You will find out

- What du'a is.
- The difference between salah and du'a.

In the glossary

Allah

Bismillah

Du'a

Madraseh

Mosque

Muhammad

Qur'an

Rak'ah

Ramadan

Salah

Surah

Tasbih

There are many occasions in life when a Muslim might want, or need, to offer up additional prayers to those laid down for salah. These occasions might include:

- During Ramadan. During this month of fasting, a Muslim's thoughts turn naturally to Allah and so saying some extra prayers is often helpful.

- When a long and difficult journey is about to be undertaken.

- After a particular blessing has been received from Allah, such as recovery from a serious illness, the birth of a baby, the end of a difficult time, the opening of a new business, etc.

- When someone is in need of help, forgiveness or guidance.

Sometimes a Muslim might use a set prayer or a passage from the Qur'an as a **du'a**. At other times, however, he might just pray as he feels that he needs to. Unlike salah, there is no set time for du'a prayers – these prayers can be of any length and offered up anywhere. Also, unlike salah, du'a prayers can be in the worshipper's own language.

Like everything else in life, prayer needs to be worked at. As the Qur'an explains:

A *"Attend regularly to your prayers, including the middle prayer, and stand up with all devotion before God."*

Qur'an. Surah 2.239

One of the main purposes of children attending a madraseh is that they learn how to pray.

TASBIH

We have already come across the tasbih in unit 4. Muslims sometimes hold a string of prayer beads between their fingers as they are praying. Each bead represents one of the 99 different Names of Allah. After performing the different rak'ahs, a Muslim may decide to praise Allah using the beads. After each bead, he or she will say, 'Glory be to Allah', 'Thanks be to Allah' or 'Allah is great'.

Muslims may pray to Allah about everything. At the same time, they always remind themselves that He knows everything about everybody. There are no secrets where Allah is concerned. As Muhammad said:

B *"You should worship Allah as if you are seeing Him; for He sees you, even if you do not see him."*

Hadith

BISMILLAH

As we will see in unit 16, some children have a special ceremony when they reach their 4th birthday. This ceremony is called the **bismillah**. Bismillah simply means, 'In the name of Allah' and the ceremony involves the child learning the words that begin all but one of the **surahs** in the Qur'an – "In the name of Allah, the gracious, the merciful."

Before this ceremony, the child learns how to say each word of the Arabic correctly and also how to pray. Whether or not each child has been through the bismillah ceremony, they begin to attend their local **madraseh** at the mosque. It is here that most of their religious education will be carried out.

OVER TO **YOU** ▶▶▶

1 Imagine that you are a Muslim. Describe three occasions on which you might feel that it is necessary to offer up du'a prayers.

2 Why might a Muslim worshipper have a tasbih, prayer beads, in his hands?

Prayer beads in a mosque ready for people to use in their prayers.

19

THE HAJJ

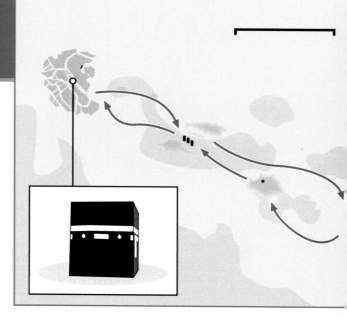

You will find out

- The meaning of the words 'Hajj' and 'ihram'.
- How pilgrims are expected to behave on the Hajj.
- The different parts of the Hajj and the importance of the Kab'ah.

In the glossary

Abraham

Allah

Hajj

Heaven

Ihram

Ka'bah

Madinah

Muhammad

Makkah

Qur'an

The word 'Hajj' means 'to undertake a journey with a definite purpose'. The pilgrimage to the city of Makkah, which almost every Muslim undertakes, is called the Hajj. Each healthy Muslim goes on the Hajj once during their lifetime. Only those who are too old, sick, disabled or poor are excused from the Hajj.

The Hajj is a deeply spiritual experience. During it, pilgrims visit Makkah and Madinah, the two most important cities in Islam. They experience the blessing of travelling, praying and having fellowship with two million other pilgrims [see Extract A].

A *"There were all kinds of people on the Hajj – men and women, black and white, rich and poor, young and old. Yet we were all brothers and sisters. We had all gone on this spiritual journey to renew our commitment to Allah. The great joy for me was to travel with so many fellow believers from many different parts of the world."*

Rasim, 34 year old Muslim, on returning from the Hajj

IHRAM

The Hajj takes place during the twelfth month of the Muslim calendar. On the outskirts of the city of Makkah, pilgrims enter a holy state – **ihram** – and this involves wearing special clothes:

- Men and boys wear two white, unsewn cotton sheets. One is tied around the waist and the other draped over the shoulder.
- Women and girls wear a long dress and a head-covering. Veils are forbidden.

In addition:

CHECK IT OUT

On the Hajj, pilgrims are forbidden to...

- use any perfume or soap.
- wear any jewellery, although women can wear their wedding ring.
- have any sexual relations.
- cut their hair or nails.
- kill any living thing, including plants.

All of these preparations put the pilgrim in a right mind to undertake the Hajj.

THE HAJJ

As soon as the pilgrim reaches Makkah, he or she heads towards the **Ka'bah**. This is the most sacred shrine in Islam. They walk seven times around the shrine in an anti-clockwise direction, saying a prayer on each circuit. They attempt to kiss the Black Stone in the Ka'bah, although the crush of pilgrims may prevent this.

The next part of the Hajj is called the Sa'y. They walk seven times between the two hills of Marwa and Safa. This reminds pilgrims of Hajar, Abraham's wife, who ran between the two hills in search of water for her son.

Pilgrims then travel to the plain of Arafat and the Mount of Mercy, where Muhammad preached his last sermon. The pilgrims stand here to pray from noon until sunset. This is the most important part of the Hajj.

Before ending the Hajj, the pilgrims go on to Mina, where they spend three days. On each day, they throw seven stones at each of the three pillars. The pillars symbolise the devil.

AFTER THE HAJJ

The Hajj is now over and pilgrims return to Makkah to walk for a last time around the Ka'bah. Some of them visit the tomb of Muhammad in Madinah. Others return home to share their blessings with friends and relations.

THE KA'BAH

The Qur'an says that the Ka'bah was first built by Abraham and his son, Ishma'il. Later, Muhammad cleared hundreds of idols out of the Ka'bah. From then onwards, it was only used for the worship of Allah. Muslims believe that it lies directly under the throne of Allah in **heaven**.

During the Hajj, the Ka'bah is covered by a large, black cloth. At the end of each Hajj, the cloth is cut up into small pieces and sold to pilgrims as a memento of their pilgrimage.

OVER TO **YOU** ▶▶▶

1 If someone who was not a Muslim was to ask you what the meaning of the Hajj was, what would you say to them?

2 a) What was the first thing that Rasim noticed on his pilgrimage?

   b) What did he discover about the purpose of everyone that he met on the pilgrimage?

   c) Why do you think he felt 'great joy' on the pilgrimage?

Makkah, showing the Kab'ah with pilgrims.

THE DAY OF JUDGEMENT

You will find out

- The link between this life and the life to come.
- About the coming Day of Judgement.
- About heaven and hell.

In the glossary

Allah

Five Pillars

Hadith

Heaven

Hell

Muhammad

Prophet

Qur'an

Islam teaches that each person only has one life and will be judged on how they have lived it. They will be judged on how well they have followed:

- The teaching of the Five Pillars. We have already discovered what the Five Pillars of Islam are [unit 5]. These are the test of each Muslim's faithfulness to Allah.
- The teaching of the Qur'an.
- The example set by the Prophet Muhammad shown in the Hadith.

This is what the Qur'an says:

A *"He created life and death in order to test which of you does good works."*

Qur'an. Surah 67.2

By following the teaching of the Five Pillars, the Qur'an and the example set by Muhammad, a person knows that they can make the difficult choices of life correctly. One other consideration, however, is also important – the motive behind every action:

B *"If a person intends to do something wrong and does not do it this is a good deed. If a person intends to do something wrong and does it this is a bad deed. If a person intends to do a good deed but cannot manage to carry it out, this is a good deed. If a person intends to do a good deed and carries it out, this is equal to ten good deeds."*

Hadith

THE DAY OF JUDGEMENT

The shattering events of the Day of Judgement will take place at a time known only to Allah. On that day, life as we know it will end and a new order will begin. On the Day of Judgement:

- All graves will be opened.
- All of the dead will be brought back to life.
- All people will stand before Allah, their Judge.
- Those who have died in battle for Allah will pass directly into heaven.
- The deeds of everyone will be weighed in the balance.

Allah's judgement on them will be shown by the presentation of a book. If the book is placed in their right hand, they will be counted as blessed and go directly to heaven. If the book is placed in their left hand, they will be counted among the damned and sent to **hell**.

OVER TO YOU ▶▶▶

1 There are three tests by which a Muslim will be judged. What are they?
2 You have been asked to talk to your class about the Muslim belief in a Day of Judgement. Write down six points that you would make in your talk.
3 Write down three things that Muslims believe about:
   a) Heaven   b) Hell

Muslims believe that hell is a place of real and eternal torment.

HEAVEN

Three groups of people will find themselves in heaven:

- Those who believe in Allah and have lived charitable and faithful lives.
- Those who have been persecuted for Allah's sake.
- Those who have fought and died on Allah's side.

The imagery of heaven with its rivers, plants and trees is much appreciated by those who have spent their lives in desert areas. The real joy of heaven, however, is to experience the continual presence of Allah. This is what true Muslims long for and which will last forever.

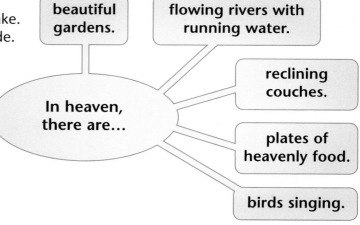

In heaven, there are...
- beautiful gardens.
- flowing rivers with running water.
- reclining couches.
- plates of heavenly food.
- birds singing.

HELL

The wicked will pass over a very narrow bridge and fall into hell. Of these people, the Qur'an says:

C *"Fear the fire of hell whose fuel is people who disbelieve."*　　　　Qur'an. Surah 2.24

The suffering of those in hell is eternal. Hell is a place of scorching flame under the earth's crust. Those in hell are chained up with hot winds, boiling water and black smoke around them. They stay in hell forever.

THE UMMAH

You will find out

- The meaning of the word 'Ummah'.
- The signs of Ummah.

In the glossary

Hajj

Ka'bah

Makkah

Mosque

Muhammad

Prophet

Qiblah

Qur'an

Rak'ah

Salah

Ummah

Zakah

'Ummah' is an important word in Islam. The photograph of Muslims together shows you what the word means. It was first used to describe the Prophet Muhammad's companions in Madinah. It now describes the worldwide community of Muslims and expresses the spiritual unity of this community.

THE SIGNS OF UMMAH

At the heart of Islam there are common activities which involve all Muslims. Among these activities are:

- The Friday Prayers, when all male Muslims make every attempt to be present in the mosque at noon. The prayer rak'ahs are an expression of their unity one with another as they stand shoulder to shoulder to pray.
- During their prayers, another expression of their unity is also important. Everyone prays facing the Ka'bah in Makkah. The Ka'bah, the holiest shrine in Islam, is a symbol of that unity which links together Muslims everywhere. The direction of Makkah in a mosque is called the **Qiblah**. You will find out more about the mosque and its importance in Muslim worship in units 23 and 24.
- Learning to recite and understand the holy book, the Qur'an, which all Muslims share together. Verses from the Qur'an, recited in Arabic, form an important part of the worship of all Muslims. You will find out more about the Qur'an and the part that it plays in Muslim devotion in units 12 and 13.
- The language of Arabic unites Muslims throughout the world. This is why the language is used for all parts of the salah as well as for reading the Qur'an.
- The unity which all Muslims feel when they go on pilgrimage together on the Hajj to Makkah. On this journey, everyone, rich and poor, is equal. All pilgrims show this by wearing the same simple clothes. On the Hajj, an animal is killed and the meat is shared with those who are too poor to buy an animal for themselves. You found out more about the Hajj in unit 9.
- The giving of money to the poor and to other good causes. This duty, called zakah, is a way of sharing one's wealth with others. This reminds Muslims that all of their wealth is a gift from Allah and so belongs to everyone.

This page shows English and Arabic script from the Qur'an. Learning Arabic is an expression of Muslim unity.

TAKE TIME TO THINK

Why do you think that Islam places such a high value on the unity of the Muslim community?

OVER TO **YOU** ▶▶▶

1 How does the pilgrimage of the Hajj to Makkah express the unity that exists between all Muslims?

2 How do Muslims express their unity with each other?

3 As we have seen, Ummah is one of the most important things in a Muslim's life. It is the basis of many ahadith [plural of hadith]. Here are three examples:

A *"Each of you is a mirror of his brother; if you see something wrong in your brother, you must tell him to get rid of it."*

B *"Believers are part of a building to one another – each part supporting the others."*

C *"None of you can be a believer unless he loves for his brother what he loves for himself."*

a) What do you think it means to call each Muslim "a mirror of his brother"?

b) Describe two ways in which a Muslim is expected to support other members of the faith.

c) What do you love for yourself? Could you love the same things for other people?

You will find out

- The meaning of the word 'Qur'an'.

- Some of the teachings of the Qur'an.

In the glossary

Allah

Angle Jibril

Muhammad

Prophet

Qur'an

Surah

Muslims believe that the Qur'an is so special that they need to spend their lifetime memorising and understanding it.

Muslims love and respect their holy book, the Qur'an, very much. The name itself means 'recitation' and this is important in two ways:

- The words of the Qur'an were originally recited [read aloud] to the Prophet Muhammad by the Angel Jibril.

- The beauty of the Qur'an is only fully appreciated when it is read aloud. Reading the Qur'an out loud is a central part of every Muslim act of worship.

THE QUR'AN

There are 114 **surahs** or chapters in the Qur'an. All of them, except one, begin with the words: "In the Name of God, the Compassionate, the Merciful." Each of the surahs are believed to have been revealed to Muhammad by Allah. They could not have been created by human hands or the human mind.

The surahs are not written down in the order in which they were revealed to Muhammad. They are written down in the Qur'an in the order in which they were collected together by Muhammad's companions. Within 20 years, the Qur'an was written down as one book.

Each surah has its own title. The title is taken from some word, or theme, in the surah. So, for example, the second surah is called 'The Cow' because it contains a story about Musa [Moses] asking the people to sacrifice a cow.

The surah which Muslims know best is the first. They recite it every day. You can read this surah in Extract A:

A "*Praise be to God, Lord of the Universe,*
The Compassionate, the Merciful,
Sovereign of the Day of Judgement!
You alone we worship, and to You alone we turn for help.
Guide us to the straight path,
The path of those whom You have favoured,
Not of those who have incurred Your wrath [made you angry],
Nor of those who have gone astray."

Qur'an. Surah 1

OVER TO **YOU** ▶▶▶

1 Imagine that you are a Muslim. Write down one or two feelings that you are likely to have about the Qur'an.

2 Explain why the Qur'an has been given its name.

3 Read surah 1 from the Qur'an in Extract A.

   a) Several titles and names are given to Allah in this extract. Make a list of them and try to explain the meaning of two of them.

   b) What does each worshipper ask Allah to do for them?

THE TEACHINGS OF THE QUR'AN

The teachings of the Qur'an guide every Muslim. They tell them how Allah expects them to live day by day as they submit themselves to His will. These teachings also explain how they can prepare themselves to stand before Allah on the Day of Judgement without fear. For example, it tells them that they should:

- share their wealth and knowledge freely.

- treat every human being with great respect.

- look after the widows, orphans and the sick within the community.

- not engage in any activities, such as drinking alcohol, taking drugs or gambling, which will damage the mind.

- help to pay the debts of the poor and free the slaves from their captivity.

Children are taught Arabic and the teachings of the Qur'an from the age of four onwards.

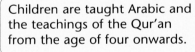

TAKE TIME TO THINK

Why do you think that each Muslim wants to have a guide to show them how they are expected to live day by day?

USING THE QUR'AN

You will find out

- About Muslim schools and religious education.

- About learning the Qur'an.

- The importance of Friday Prayer.

In the glossary

Allah

Hadith

Imam

Khutbah

Madraseh

Mosque

Muhammad

Prophet

Qur'an

Shi'ite Muslims

The Prophet Muhammad said this about the Qur'an:

A *"The best of you is he who has learnt and then taught it."*

Muslims make every effort to learn and understand Allah's message in the Qur'an. Many of them also teach the Qur'an to others – especially the young.

MUSLIM SCHOOLS

Each mosque has its own school, or madraseh, in which young Muslims learn about their faith. In Britain, they usually go to the madraseh after they have attended their day school. There they learn about their faith and the language of Arabic for a few hours every day.

Muslim boys and girls start their religious education at an early age. They are encouraged to continue with that education when they become teenagers. Many of them stay with it until they become teachers themselves.

OVER TO YOU ▶▶▶

1 What is a madraseh?
2 Why are Muslim children sent to a madraseh and when do they attend it?

Muslims start their religious education early. They try to commit as much of the Qur'an to memory as possible.

LEARNING THE QUR'AN

The vast majority of Muslims are not Arabs and so Arabic is not their native tongue. They read the Qur'an in translation in their own language. At the same time, however, as the Qur'an has been translated into many languages so it always loses some of its beauty in the translation. To counter this, Muslims try to understand the meaning and spirit of Allah's revelation.

FRIDAY PRAYERS

Friday Prayers, which begin at noon, are important to Muslim men throughout the world. Taking part in Friday Prayers is the most important act of worship for all Muslim men. Before the prayers begin, the imam gives a short talk and this is called the **khutbah**.

The imam is the leader of the prayers in a mosque. For Shi'ite Muslims, the imam is the spiritual leader of the community. The imam who leads the prayers must:

* have a good understanding of Islam.

* carry the respect of his fellow Muslims.

* be known for his own holiness of life and that of his family.

* have studied both the Qur'an and the Hadith.

In the khutbah, the imam explains a passage from the Qur'an or a story about the Prophet Muhammad. All Muslims have a great deal of respect for the Qur'an. No one is allowed to talk, eat, drink or make a noise while it is being read in public. When it is not being used, the holy book must be kept covered and placed up high in a room. It must never touch the ground, whether it is being read or not. This is why Muslims place it on a stool when they are reading from it.

OVER TO YOU ▶▶▶

Here are three quotations from the Qur'an. Read them carefully:

B "*He [Allah] has revealed to you the Book with the Truth...*"
Qur'an. Surah 3.2

C "*This Qur'an could not have been devised by any but God.*"
Qur'an. Surah 10.38

D "*This [Qur'an] is insight from your Lord, and a guidance and a mercy to people that believe. And when the Qur'an is recited listen to it with attention.*"
Qur'an. Surah 7.203-4

3 According to these quotations:

a) Who has given the Qur'an to mankind?

b) What is 'the Book'?

c) Could the Qur'an have been written by human beings?

d) Where did the Qur'an come from?

e) What does the Qur'an offer those who believe?

TAKE TIME TO THINK

Why do you think that Muslims believe that it is important that they learn to read and study the Qur'an in its original language?

You will find out

- About the Hadith.
- About the Sirah.
- About the Sunnah.

In the glossary

Allah

Hadith

Muhammad

Prophet

Qur'an

Ramadan

Sunnah

Sunni Muslims

THE HADITH

The Hadith is a very important collection of the sayings of the Prophet Muhammad. These sayings were collected together after his death by his closest followers. They expand and illustrate many of the verses in the Qur'an and are easier to understand than the Qur'an. They give everyday illustrations to set beside the teachings of the holy book.

When these sayings were first recorded, great care was taken to trace them right back to the actual words of Muhammad. They cover all kinds of topics including fasting, pilgrimage, prayer, social life between Muslims and human relationships.

Here are five examples from the Hadith:

A *"He is not a believer who eats his fill while his neighbour goes without food."*

B *"When people see evil but make no effort to change it, Allah will inflict His punishment on all of them."*

C *"A man came to the Prophet and asked, 'Who, among all people, is most worthy of my good company?' The Prophet replied, 'Your mother.' The man asked, 'Who next?' The Prophet said, 'Your mother.' The man asked again, 'Who next?' Again the Prophet said, 'Your mother.' Only next did he say, 'Your father.'"*

D *"The two Muslims who meet and shake hands with each other are forgiven before they separate."*

E *"Be in the world as if you are a stranger or a wayfarer."*

THE SIRAH

Muslims regard the Hadith as being only slightly less important than the words of the Qur'an. The Sirah [accounts of the Prophet's life] is also valued very highly and used by Muslims as a guide in their everyday living.

Many Muslim customs are based on the Sirah, including the custom of breaking the fast of Ramadan. The information that we have about the life of the Prophet and also many of the stories that we have about his early life also come from the Sirah.

THE SUNNAH

The Hadith and the Sirah together form the Sunnah. This does not exist as a single book. Instead it is the total source of everything that is known about the Prophet Muhammad and this is how Muslims see it.

The largest group of Muslims, the Sunni, accept the Sunnah as the foundation on which they build both their faith and their life.

TAKE TIME TO THINK

The ahadith are short and memorable statements to express Muslim beliefs. Make up three similar statements which express beliefs that you hold about life.

OVER TO **YOU** ▶▶▶

1 If you were given a copy of the Hadith, what would you expect to find in it?

2 Working with your partner, choose two of the ahadith in this spread and work out what you think they mean. Then either:
   a) Draw a picture to which one of the ahadith could act as a caption OR
   b) Write a story or a play which would make the same moral point as your chosen hadith.

3 a) What is the Sunnah?
   b) Why is the Sunnah so important to Sunni Muslims?

FAMILY LIFE

You will find out

- The importance of Muslim family life.
- The responsibilities of parents.
- The responsibilities of children.

In the glossary

Allah

Muhammad

Prophet

Qur'an

Ramadan

Muslims believe that family life is extremely important. It is the foundation on which Muslim society is built. Family life is where the most important things in life, especially family values and the need to care for each other, are taught. Children learn how they must behave in the family. It is in the family home that children learn their first lessons about the religion of Islam. Children also discover how to look after themselves in the safe and secure atmosphere that family life provides.

THE MUSLIM FAMILY

A Muslim family includes everyone who is related to everyone else – no matter how distant that relationship might be. This encourages everyone to care for everyone else. The Prophet Muhammad said:

A *"The best of you are those who are kind to your family."*

Hadith

THE DUTIES OF PARENTS

Both the mother and the father have a duty to bring up their children to be good Muslims. This means teaching them about Islam from a very young age and setting them a good example both inside and outside the home. Also in the family home:

CHECK IT OUT

In the family, children learn...

- stories about the Prophet Muhammad.
- short passages from the Qur'an.
- the correct way to pray.
- the correct way to dress.
- how to conduct themselves in public and private.
- how to fast during Ramadan.

The mother's job is to look after her children from day to day. Muhammad said that every mother should be a good friend to her children. She should be warm, affectionate, generous and fair in the way she treats them. The father's main responsibility is to provide for his children. He must see that they never go without anything that they need. The mother and father may carry different responsibilities but both of them are equally important in a happy family.

The responsibilities that mothers and fathers carry remain until their children marry. Their final responsibility is to find a suitable marriage partner for their children.

TAKE TIME TO THINK

What do you think:
a) Parents owe to their children?
b) Children owe to their parents?

Each member of a Muslim family has clear responsibilities to the others.

THE DUTIES OF CHILDREN

Muslim children have the responsibility of obeying and respecting their parents for the whole of their lives. It does not matter how old their parents are or how old the children are. The Qur'an says that serving Allah comes first but serving one's parents is next in order of importance. It further says:

B *"Your Lord has ordered that you… show kindness to your parents. If either or both of them attain old age in your dwelling, show them no signs of impatience, nor rebuke them but speak to them kind words. Treat them with humility and tenderness and say: 'Lord be merciful to them. They nursed me when I was an infant.'"*

Qur'an. Surah 17.23-24

Muslims today take this to mean that it is disrespectful to put elderly relatives into an old people's home to be cared for by strangers. Instead, Muslim families care for their elderly members at home with everyone showing them the loving attention that they deserve.

OVER TO **YOU** ▶▶▶

1   What do you think are three differences between Muslim family life and your own life at home? [If you are a Muslim, compare your family life with that of your friends.]
2   Muslim parents have a responsibility to bring their children up as good Muslims but what is a 'good Muslim'?
3   Write down three items in each of these columns:

Muslim father's duties	Muslim mother's duties

UNIT 16
CHILDHOOD

You will find out

- The importance of a birth of a baby in a Muslim family.
- About the aqiqah ceremony.
- About the bismillah ceremony.

In the glossary

Adhan

Allah

Angel Jibril

Aqiqah

Bismillah

Circumcision

Khitan

Madraseh

Mosque

Muhammad

Prophet

Qur'an

Ummah

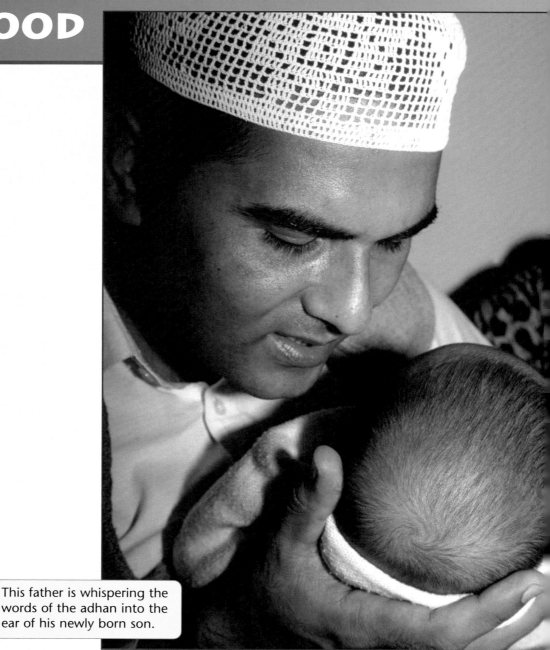

This father is whispering the words of the adhan into the ear of his newly born son.

As gifts from Allah, every newborn baby is welcomed into the Ummah – the worldwide Muslim 'family' – as soon as possible. This spiritual 'family' will support and care for it for the rest of its life.

BIRTH

As soon as possible after birth, some Muslim communities carry out the **aqiqah** ceremony. For this, the father takes the baby in his arms and whispers the adhan, the call to prayer, in his right ear. You can read the **adhan** in unit 6.

Speaking the adhan in this way to a new-born baby means that the first word that a child hears is that of Allah. Then, after the adhan has been recited, a tiny piece of sugar or date is placed on the baby's tongue by an elderly relative. This expresses the hope that the baby will grow up to be kind and considerate.

THE AQIQAH CEREMONY

This ceremony is held when a baby is seven days old. Several important things may happen at this time:

- The child's head is shaved. This symbolises the removal of all misfortune. Gold and silver equivalent to the weight of the hair is given to the poor and needy.
- A sheep or a goat may be sacrificed. A third of the animal is eaten by the family and the rest is given away to the poor.
- The child is given its name. In Islam, a person's name is very important. Many children are named after Allah, Muhammad or one of the other prophets.
- If the baby is a boy, **circumcision** will probably take place at the same time. Boys can, however, be circumcised at any time up to their tenth birthday.

THE BISMILLAH CEREMONY

In some Muslim countries, the bismillah ceremony is held when a child is exactly four years, four months and four days old. It celebrates the time when the Angel Jibril appeared to the Prophet Muhammad. It is the start of a child's religious education, when he or she learns the first sentence of the Qur'an off by heart:

A *"In the name of God, the Compassionate, the Merciful."*

Qur'an. Surah 1.1

Muslims take the religious education of their children very seriously. It begins, as we have seen, with the bismillah ceremony. It continues at the madraseh – the school in the mosque.

KHITAN

If the baby is a boy then he must be circumcised. This means cutting off the foreskin, the flap of skin at the end of the penis. The Arabic word for circumcision is **khitan**. A boy may be circumcised at the same time as the aqiqah is carried out or left for some time. Muslim parents, however, are under a religious obligation to have their sons circumcised.

OVER TO YOU ▶▶▶

1 a) Why do you think that a person's name is so important in Islam? Could there be a link between a person's name and the kind of person that they turn out to be?

   b) Why are many Muslim names derived from Allah, Muhammad or one of the prophets? What might the parents be hoping for when they choose such a name?

2 At the bismillah ceremony, some verses from the Qur'an are read to the child who then recites them [B].

B *"Recite in the name of the Lord who created – created man from clots of blood. Recite! Your Lord is the Most Bountiful One, who by the pen taught man what he did not know."*

Qur'an. Surah 96.1

   a) What happens at the bismillah ceremony?

   b) Why is the bismillah ceremony an important stage in the life of every young Muslim?

   c) Why do you think that these words are appropriate to read at this time?

TAKE TIME TO THINK

Why do you think that Muslims sacrifice an animal during the aqiqah ceremony?

You will find out

- The teaching of the Qur'an on marriage.
- About arranged marriages.
- About polygamy.
- The marriage contract and ceremony.

In the glossary

Allah

Imam

Mosque

Qur'an

Getting married in the Muslim community is simple and straightforward. The ceremony can take place anywhere although, in Britain, it is usually performed by an imam in a mosque. The wedding is not a religious ceremony. It is carried out in accordance with the laws of the country in which the couple live.

WHAT DOES THE QUR'AN EXPECT?

The Qur'an expects a couple to grow in their love for each other throughout their married life. This is Allah's intention for every man and woman [A]:

A *"He [Allah] gave you spouses [husbands and wives] from among yourselves, that you might live in peace with them, and planted love and kindness in your hearts."*

Qur'an. Surah 30.20

ARRANGED MARRIAGES

An 'arranged marriage' is one in which parents and other relations have some influence over the choice of a person's partner. Here are two comments about arranged marriage by Muslim young people:

B *"In Muslim communities, marriage is much more than the uniting of two people. It is the bringing together of two families and so many people are involved. Also, as young people, we need to use the wisdom of those older than us before making such an important decision."*

Afez

C *"I was born in England and have lived here all my life. Although some of my Muslim friends will go through an arranged marriage, it is not for me. Fortunately, my parents agree with me. They will allow me to choose my future partner – without any outside interference!"*

Jamneez

Most religions, including Islam, encourage their young people to marry within the faith.

MORE THAN ONE WIFE?

The Qur'an allows a man to have up to four wives at a time and this is called polygamy. If he does so, however, he must treat each of them equally and fairly. In practice, however, few Muslims have more than one wife and it only happens if the first wife:

- is unable to give her husband children.
- is so ill that she is unable to run the home.

TAKE TIME TO THINK

Some people argue that couples in the West meet, fall in love, marry and then fall out of love whereas Muslim couples marry first and then fall in love. What do you think?

THE MARRIAGE CONTRACT AND CEREMONY

When a Muslim couple marry, a contract is drawn up. The marriage contract states that:

- A woman can insist that her husband does not marry anyone else.
- A sum of money is paid by the husband's family – called the 'dowry' – which remains the wife's possession if the couple later divorce.

CHECK
IT OUT

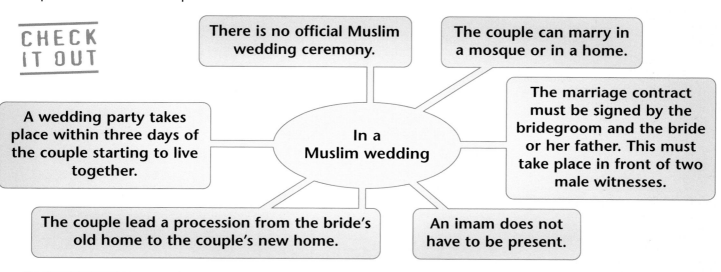

There is no official Muslim wedding ceremony.

The couple can marry in a mosque or in a home.

A wedding party takes place within three days of the couple starting to live together.

In a Muslim wedding

The marriage contract must be signed by the bridegroom and the bride or her father. This must take place in front of two male witnesses.

The couple lead a procession from the bride's old home to the couple's new home.

An imam does not have to be present.

OVER TO YOU ▶▶▶

1 Why, according to the Qur'an, did Allah give marriage to human beings?

2 Read Extracts B and C. Which of the two do you have most sympathy with? Explain your answer.

3 Explain two things that must be in a Muslim wedding contract.

4 Draw pictures of three important parts of a Muslim wedding ceremony and explain underneath what your pictures are showing.

5 As part of a wedding ceremony, the couple are asked three times if they agree to marry each other and they exchange rings. The imam, or someone else, blesses them with the words: "In the Name of God, the Compassionate, the Merciful." Why do you think:

a) The couple are asked three times if they consent to the marriage?

b) The couple exchange rings?

c) The couple are blessed in the name of Allah?

You will find out

- The example set by Muhammad.
- About Muslims – before and after death.
- About mourning in the Muslim community.

In the glossary

Allah

Hajj

Hell

Ka'bah

Makkah

Mosque

Muhammad

Prophet

Qur'an

Shahadah

THE EXAMPLE OF MUHAMMAD

As he approached death, the Prophet Muhammad reportedly said:

A *"Allah, help me through the hardship and agony of death."*

Muslims try to follow Muhammad's example as they approach death. As they believe strongly in life after death so Muslims try to approach the end of their life calmly. They believe that, after death, their souls with enter eternal life to be reunited with the souls of loved ones [B]:

B *"To God we belong and to God we will return."*

Qur'an. Surah 2.156

BEFORE AND AFTER DEATH

All Muslims hope that they will be able to recite the Shahadah before dying so that all of their sins will be forgiven. Relatives and friends gather around their bedside as the person asks the forgiveness of everyone for any sins they have committed against them. Passages are read from the Qur'an and prayers are said.

After death, the body is washed in scented water. This can be done by the husband or wife or someone of the same sex. The body is then dressed in white robes – three for a man and five for a woman. The robes are often those that the person wore on the Hajj. Then the body is taken to the mosque or an open space for the funeral prayer [C].

C *"O God, pardon this dead person; lo, Thou art the Most Forgiving, the Most Merciful."*

Muslims do not cremate their dead – the body is always buried. In Muslim countries, a coffin is not used so that the body can be in direct contact with the earth. It is laid with the right side facing Makkah and the head turned in the same direction.

CHECK IT OUT

are messengers from Allah – creatures of light who are in constant contact with human beings.

are acknowledged by human beings when they turn their heads from side to side as they are praying.

Angels...

support everyone who prays or has thoughts about Allah.

keep a record of everything that human beings do.

occasionally appear to human beings but are usually unseen.

The body is carried to the place of burial. Only males are allowed to attend this.

THE VISIT OF TWO ANGELS

The Prophet Muhammad wept when his son died. Muslims are not afraid to show their feelings and their mourning for a dead person lasts between seven days and three months.

After burial, it is believed that the grave is visited by two angels who question the dead person to see whether they are fit to enter paradise. To help the dead person answer the questions satisfactorily, mourners can recite the verse you can find in Extract D at the graveside:

D *"O male or female servant of God, remember the covenant [vow] made while leaving the world, that is the attestation [confirmation] that there is no God if not God Himself and that Muhammad was the Messenger of God, and the belief that paradise is a verity [truth], that hell is a verity, that the questioning in the grave is a verity, that the Day of Judgement shall come, there being no doubt about it – that God will bring back to life those who are in the graves, that thou hast accepted God as thy Lord, Islam as thy religion, Muhammad as thy prophet, the Qur'an as thy guide, the Ka'bah as thy direction to turn to for the service of worship and that all believers are thy brethren [brothers]. May God keep thee firm in this trial."*

OVER TO YOU ▶▶▶

1 If a Muslim says that they hope to follow the example of the Prophet Muhammad as they approach death, what do they mean?

2 What happens to comfort a Muslim in the last few hours of their life?

3 How do Muslims prepare a dead body for burial?

4 Read Extract D through carefully before answering these questions:

   a) What do you think a 'verity' is? How many verities are mentioned here and what are they?

   b) There are several characteristics of the true Muslim who can look forward to the Day of Judgement with confidence. What are they?

TAKE TIME TO THINK

As a Muslim is buried, handfuls of earth are dropped into the grave. Why do you think this is done?

39

UNIT 19
THE PLACE OF WOMEN IN ISLAM

You will find out

- The traditional roles played by men and women in Islam.
- The modern roles that many modern Muslim women play.

In the glossary

Allah

Five Pillars

Hajj

Halal

Madraseh

Mosque

Muhammad

Prophet

Qur'an

In Islam, all men and women are believed to be equal. The Qur'an addresses men as 'the believing men' and women as 'the believing women'. This is because the message of Allah as it is revealed in the Qur'an applies equally to both sexes.

WOMEN IN ISLAM

Islam teaches that men and women have been given different roles to play by Allah. At the same time, they are equal in matters of religion and the right to education. These are the traditional roles expected of men and women in Muslim societies:

CHECK IT OUT

To have children.

To create a **halal** – a good Muslim home.

To fulfil all of the Five Pillars, except the Hajj, at home.

The traditional roles of Muslim women

To bring up children to be good Muslims.

To worship Allah. Muslim women, however, are expected to look after their families even if it cuts across their religious duties.

To support his wife since Allah gave him a stronger physique [A].

To provide for his family.

To educate his sons about their religious responsibilities and to worship alongside them in the mosque.

The traditional roles of Muslim men

To make sure his children attend the madraseh.

To make sure that his children are brought up as good Muslims.

A *"Husbands are the protectors and maintainers of their wives, because Allah has given the one more strength than the other, and because they support them from their means. Therefore the righteous women are devoutly obedient and guard in the [husband's] absence what Allah have them guard."*

Qur'an. Surah 4.34

The Qur'an, then, underlines the responsibility of the Muslim man to look after his wife and family. It also underlines the responsibility of the wife to provide her husband with children and to look after them.

The Qur'an also says that women should only inherit 50% of what men inherit, showing that men are intended by Allah to look after their whole family – relations as well as closest family.

THE MODERN ROLES OF WOMEN IN ISLAM

Some Muslims believe that men and women should have equal rights and responsibilities within society. They believe that women should be able to pursue a career of their own as well as looking after their family. Many women are heavily involved, for example, in the teaching and medical fields.

They also believe that women should be allowed to pray alongside men in the mosque. This attitude is based on the teaching in the Qur'an that men and women should be equal in both religion and education. There is also evidence from the life of Muhammad that men and women prayed together in the mosque during his lifetime.

In the UK, many Muslims combine the old, traditional viewpoint with a more modern approach. Women pursue independent careers of their own but they worship at home because that fits in better with their family obligations.

B *"Modesty and faith are joined closely together; if either of them is lost, the other goes also."*

Words of Muhammad to his companions

C *"The believers, men and women, are protectors of one another. They enjoin what is just and forbid what is evil. They observe regular prayers, pay alms regularly and obey God and His messenger."*

Qur'an. Surah 9.71

OVER TO YOU ▶▶▶

1 What do you think the Qur'an means when it teaches that men and women have different roles? Give two examples in your answer.

2 Imagine that you are a Muslim father. Describe three things you would do to make sure that your children are brought up as good Muslims.

3 Describe in a paragraph the traditional roles that men and women are expected to play in Islam.

4 Why do you think that the Prophet Muhammad saw a very close link between modesty and faith in Allah? What do you think 'modesty' is?

Although both men and women pray in Islam, they do not pray side by side.

OLD AGE

You will find out

- About the extended family.
- How grandparents should be treated.
- The qualities expected from Muslims towards parents and grandparents.

In the glossary

Extended Family

Hadith

Qur'an

Old age gives Muslims the opportunity to spend time reading and studying the Qur'an.

In every community, as people grow old they need special care and help. In Muslim communities, this love is provided by the family. There are many passages in the Qur'an and the Hadith which encourage Muslims to look after their parents when they grow old. The care of old people is never passed on to someone outside the family. That would be unthinkable.

THE EXTENDED FAMILY

In some parts of the world, especially in rural areas, Muslims live in **extended families**. This means that brothers, sisters, grandparents, aunts and uncles live close together if not under the same roof and support each other.

In cities, however, it is more likely that a smaller family consisting of parents, children and sometimes grandparents will live together. Wherever they live, however, Muslim families stay in close contact with each other.

TAKE TIME TO THINK

Describe one advantage and one disadvantage which you think might come from living in an extended family.

A Muslim family breaks their fast together during Ramadan.

CELEBRATING RAMADAN

Ramadan is a holy month because the Qur'an was given at this time. This is why extra time is given to studying the Qur'an during this month. More people go to their local mosque to pray to Allah. Some Muslims actually live at the mosque for the last ten days of Ramadan so that they can read the Qur'an and pray.

Here are three comments by young Muslims about the importance to them of keeping Ramadan:

Not everyone is expected to fast. Exceptions are made for those who are very young or old, pregnant women, those who are sick and travellers – although travellers are expected to fast at some other time.

— Naseem

Everyone fasts in my family. Fasting brings the whole family together. It helps us all to learn what it is like for some people to be always hungry and thirsty. This is why the fast always ends with our family making a gift for the poor and needy.

Kamran

I first kept the fast of Ramadan when I was thirteen years old. My older brother did the same. When the month of fasting comes to an end, everyone celebrates the festival of Id-ul-Fitr. Everyone is in a very happy mood because the hardship of Ramadan has come to an end.

Nusrat

OVER TO YOU ▶▶▶

1 What is Ramadan?
2 Explain why all Muslims try to fast for the month of Ramadan.
3 Look at what Extracts A, B and C say about fasting. Write down these teachings.
4 When Muslims fast, they have to give up many things. Have you ever had to go without things that you enjoy a lot – such as television, chocolate, your computer or your friends – for some time? Write about it or imagine what it would be like if you had to do without them.
5 Read the comments about keeping Ramadan. Write down three things that you can learn about keeping the fast from them.

You will find out

- The meaning of the word 'mosque'.
- The importance of the mosque.
- The other uses to which the mosque is put.

In the glossary

Allah

Madraseh

Minaret

Mosque

Muhammad

Prophet

Qur'an

Salah

Wudu

The Prophet Muhammad encouraged Muslims to pray in a mosque whenever possible because it is a meeting place for people to share news, swap opinions and support each other. It is also a place where Muslims 'prostrate themselves' – where they bow down to worship Allah. The word 'mosque' means 'a place of prostration'.

THERE ARE MOSQUES EVERYWHERE

There are mosques to be found everywhere in the world. This is because a Muslim community will try to build a mosque as soon as it is established. A mosque should be built as soon as there are 40 male Muslims in the area.

The Prophet Muhammad said:

A *"Prayer performed in company is twenty-seven times better than prayer performed alone."*

This is the reason why Muslim males pray in a mosque as often as possible. At the same time, Muslims know that they can worship Allah in any clean place if they cannot reach a mosque or are travelling.

Some mosques are very large and are built to take thousands of worshippers. Others are much smaller and may originally have been used as a house or a church.

The largest mosque in the UK has been built in Regents Park, London. It is attended by people of different races and nationalities from around the world. It has a dome, a **minaret** and a courtyard as do all purpose-built mosques. The design was chosen after a competition and paid for by Muslims around the world.

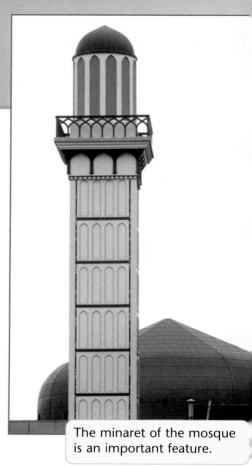

The minaret of the mosque is an important feature.

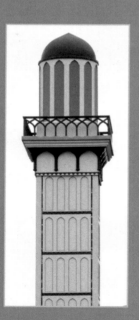

OVER TO **YOU** ▶▶▶

1 The Qur'an says that it is best to: "...worship along with those who bow their heads..."
   a) What do you think that this means?
   b) How does this tie in with what the Prophet Muhammad said in Extract A?
2 A Muslim said, "Whenever I see a mosque I think of Bilal." Find out what he meant.
3 Describe four ways in which a mosque may be used apart from as a place of prayer.

OTHER USES FOR A MOSQUE

Mosques are not just places of prayer. They are also used as:

- A school. This is where children and adults can learn Arabic and study the Qur'an. From the age of four, children attend the madraseh to be taught.
- A Law Court. Matters concerning Islamic law are often decided in the local mosque.
- A location for religious celebrations. Celebrations of births and marriages are often held in the mosque as are gatherings after funerals.
- A community centre. This is where people meet to discuss matters that affect their daily lives. This is particularly important where people are living in a country like the UK where the majority of people are not Muslims.

RUNNING WATER

It is essential for a mosque to have a supply of running water. In older mosques, this may take the form of a fountain or a tap in the courtyard, but modern buildings have washrooms with rows of taps. This is where Muslims perform wudu, the washing before prayer. Men and women have separate washing facilities.

TAKE TIME TO THINK

A mosque is often very beautiful. It provides a place of peace and quiet in a noisy and busy world. Design a room in your school or house that could be a place of quiet. Describe how you would decorate the room and what you would put in it. Design a poster to put on the door showing what the room is for.

PRAYING ON THE STREET

Salah [prayer] has to be performed five times a day – at dawn, noon, late afternoon, dusk and after dark. In Muslim countries, it is normal for people to pray at their school or place of work. They may spread out their prayer mat in a park or the local bazaar.

Sometimes, for Friday Prayers or on special occasions, the number of worshippers is too large to be housed in the mosque. In Muslim countries, on these occasions it is common to see worshippers praying on the streets surrounding the mosque.

There are no pictures or furniture inside a mosque

49

INSIDE A MOSQUE

You will find out

- About the prayer room in a mosque.
- About the mihrab and minbar.
- The importance of the mosque in the life of a young Muslim.

In the glossary

Allah

Imam

Makkah

Mihrab

Minbar

Mosque

Muhammad

Prophet

Qiblah

Qur'an

Wudu

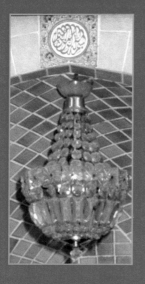

On entering a mosque, Muslims remove their shoes and place them in a shoe rack outside the door. This is a way of showing respect to Allah. The Muslim worshipper then washes themselves so that they are fit to offer worship to Allah – called wudu. Just inside the door of the mosque there is a row of clocks. These show the times at which prayers will be offered each day. The times vary according to the country and the season as the time for prayer depends on the position of the sun.

THE PRAYER ROOM

There is no furniture in the main prayer room of a mosque. The floor is usually covered by a patterned carpet. Green is a likely colour for the carpet as that was the favourite colour of Muhammad.

Individual worshippers often bring their own prayer mat with them which they lay out on the carpet. This often has the picture of a famous mosque or the holy city of Makkah on it. Using a prayer mat helps worshippers:

- To form neat rows as they pray.
- To pray facing the city of Makkah – an important requirement.
- To understand that each worshipper is equal in the sight of Allah.

Pictures of any kind are strictly forbidden in a mosque. Muhammad told his followers that such pictures of Allah or the Prophet himself were blasphemous – an insult to Allah. The danger was that people might worship them rather than the reality behind them.

THE MIHRAB

In the main room of a mosque, there is an alcove or arch which is set into one wall of the building. This shows the **qiblah**, the direction of Makkah. This is called the **mihrab**. The alcove is often beautifully decorated. It may contain texts from the Qur'an. The prayer leader usually stands in front of it as he leads the worshippers in their prayers.

THE MINBAR

The **minbar** stands at the front of a mosque, to the right-hand side of the mihrab. This is a raised platform on which the imam stands when he delivers his address during Friday Prayers. Some minbars are highly decorated while others are just a simple platform or a small flight of steps.

The minbar fulfils a simple function in the mosque. It raises the imam so that worshippers can see him clearly and hear what he is saying more easily.

The minbar in a mosque.

Worshippers know that, when they stand facing the mihrab in a mosque, they are facing Makkah.

OVER TO **YOU** ▶▶▶

1 Time for a little detective work! Try to find out why:

   a) There is no furniture in the main room of a mosque.

   b) The floor of a mosque is almost always covered by a carpet.

2 Using the information and the photographs in this spread to help you, write a letter or send a text message to a friend describing the inside of a mosque.

3 What do worshippers know if they stand facing the minbar while they are praying?

4 Describe what you know about:

   a) The mihrab

   b) The minbar

THE MOSQUE AND ME – YASMIN'S VIEWPOINT

Yasmin is a teenager who lives with her family in Oldham.

"I spend quite a lot of time in my local mosque. I go with my friends on Saturday morning and at least one evening after school during the week. Whilst there, I find out more about the Qur'an as well as learning Arabic. I would love to be able to read the Qur'an in its original language. At the moment, I can only read parts of the holy book in Arabic but I intend to continue with my lessons when I become an adult. The Prophet Muhammad said that the best thing is to learn the Qur'an – and then to teach others."

TAKE TIME TO THINK

How would you feel if you were sent to a religious school after your ordinary school day and at weekends? Would you think that it was a great burden? What would make you feel that it was very worthwhile?

You will find out

- Some reasons why Muslims have come to live in Britain.
- Some of the problems that Muslims living in the UK encounter.

In the glossary

Halal

Imam

Mosque

Qur'an

Muslims have been living in the UK for at least 200 years and at least 2 million are currently living in Britain. They are made up of people who:

- Have emigrated to this country as Muslims and have become part of the local Muslim community.
- Have become Muslims while they have been in the UK. Some of them have been converted to Islam while they have been at university.

Many Muslims living in Britain have come from countries where Islam is the main religion. Coming to live in a country where Islam is a minority religion has caused them many problems. Islam encourages its followers to live a distinctive way of life and this sometimes conflicts with the life-style of the people around them.

Here are four areas in which there has been conflict in the past:

1 MEDICAL SERVICES

In this country, doctors and nurses can be either sex and they will treat people of both sexes. Muslims, however, are embarrassed when a man is treated by a woman doctor and vice versa. When a Muslim is admitted to hospital as a patient, this can cause problems – as patients cannot choose the doctor who treats them.

Even on a more practical level there can be problems when a Muslim falls ill. Muslims, for example, are only allowed to eat halal meat and this is often not available in hospital. Some hospitals, however, are now trying to meet the needs of members of different religions.

2 TIME TO PRAY

Muslims are expected to pray five times a day and, for this, they need somewhere to wash. If they work in the open air, or are travelling, this can mean praying in front of other people. Such people will often not realise what is happening – or its importance to Muslims. Men will also need to be able to take time off to go to Friday Prayers.

OVER TO YOU ▶▶▶

1 Is there a mosque close to where you live? If so, try to arrange for the imam to visit your class or arrange a visit to the mosque. Plan beforehand the questions that you would like to ask.

2 What reasons can you think of why someone should want to 'convert' to Islam?

3 Why might a Muslim have a problem if he or she is admitted to hospital?

4 You are the headmaster or headmistress of a school. How do you think you should make allowances for the Muslim pupils in your school?

5 If possible, try to talk with a Muslim living in the UK about some of the issues raised in this lesson.

TAKE TIME TO THINK

Working with your partner, make a list of the problems that you think a Muslim might have in following their religion in the UK. How do you think that someone who is not a Muslim might try to make life easier for them?

There are many halal shops to meet the needs of Muslims.

3 DRESS

The Qur'an tells Muslims that they, both male and female, should dress decently. For women, this means that only their face and hands should be visible. Men should be covered between their waist and knees.

This can cause a problem, in particular, for girls. The rule is that they should, from the age of twelve onwards, keep their legs, arms and head covered. It is particularly difficult when they do P.E. at school and go swimming.

4 BOY/GIRL RELATIONSHIPS

Once they become teenagers, Muslim boys and girls are not expected to mix together. As you can imagine, this can cause a problem in a mixed school. Muslim boys and girls going out together is not expected. Muslims do not believe that it is necessary because, when it comes to choosing a marriage partner, the parents are heavily involved. Many young Muslims accept this as a good idea. Others, though, want to be like their non-Muslim friends and this can cause problems with parents.

The need to pray regularly can cause problems for some Muslims.

THE 'HAVES' AND THE 'HAVE-NOTS'

You will find out

- The division between the rich and the poor in today's world.

- The attitude of Islam towards wealth.

- The teaching of the Qur'an about sharing wealth.

In the glossary

Allah

Hadith

Muhammad

Qur'an

Sadaqah

Zakah

We live in a very unfair and unequal world. It is split between the wealthy developed world and the poor developing world. Extract A, taken from the United Nations Declaration of Human Rights, shows living in such an unequal world denies to 3 out of every 4 people in the world a basic human right:

A *"… freedom from fear and want has been proclaimed as the highest aspiration of the common people…"*

United Nations Declaration of Human Rights

ISLAM, WEALTH AND POVERTY

The teaching of Islam about wealth and poverty is very clear. The poor people in the world are the responsibility of the rich and wealthy. The rich have been blessed by Allah but only so that they can share their wealth with the poor, especially widows and orphans. Part of a rich person's wealth belongs to the poor anyway:

B *"In the wealth is the share of the beggars and the deprived."*

Qur'an. Surah 70.25

The consequences of living a selfish life and not sharing with others are very serious. The selfish person who keeps all his wealth and does not share with those in need places himself outside the Muslim community. As the Hadith says:

C *"He who eats and drinks while his brother goes hungry is not one of us."*

This is the kind of wealth that the Qur'an warns people against.

SHARING WITH THOSE IN NEED

There are two ways in which a Muslim can share his wealth with those who are in need:

- The Qur'an teaches that a worker should be paid a wage which enables them to enjoy the same standard of living as their employer. This ideal, Muslims believe, could be the starting point for solving the problem of world poverty. Poverty stems from rulers and employers who are selfish and greedy. The only answer to poverty in the world is to establish peace and justice on principles that are found in the Qur'an:

> D **"**_Those who spend their wealth in Allah's way are like a grain of corn which brings forth seven ears, each bearing a hundred grains. Allah gives plenty to whom He pleases. He is generous and knowing._**"**
>
> Qur'an. Surah 2.261

- Everything that a person has he has received from Allah. Wealth needs to be 'purified' and a person does this by giving generously to those in need. There are two ways that a Muslim can do this – by paying zakah and by paying **sadaqah**. You will find out the difference between the two by looking at unit 27.

OVER TO YOU ▶▶▶

1 Extract A suggests that the most important of all human rights is freedom from want and fear. Do you agree with this? Do you and your friends enjoy freedom from want and fear? Does everyone?

2 Muhammad was particularly concerned about the needs of orphans and widows. Carry out some research to discover why he was particularly concerned about the welfare of these two groups.

TAKE TIME TO THINK

The Qur'an says that some of us have been given wealth so that we can share it with others. Do you think that the poor have a 'right' to share your wealth? If so, how will you try to share it with them?

The Qur'an teaches that Allah has given enough for everyone to share.

ZAKAH AND SADAQAH

You will find out

- The importance of paying zakah.

- The spiritual blessing of paying zakah.

- The differences between zakah and sadaqah.

In the glossary

Allah

Five Pillars

Hadith

Heaven

Mosque

Muhammad

Qur'an

Sadaqah

Zakah

Allah's wish is for society to be fair and equal. To bring this about, He calls on all Muslims to pay zakah. Giving money to the poor is one of the Five Pillars of Islam. The word itself means 'purify' and, by paying it, Muslims are cleansing themselves from selfishness and a love of money – both of which are sins.

In Islam, compassion and generosity are very important. Muhammad was an orphan himself. The Qur'an says that Allah helped Muhammad as an orphan so Muslims should help orphans and others who need their support.

PAYING ZAKAH

Paying zakah is a spiritual act. The word itself means 'purity'. Muslims believe that they do not own anything since everything has been lent to them by Allah. As Allah has given wealth to them, so every Muslim must give generously to those in need.

At the end of each year, every Muslim must give 2.5% of his or her savings as zakah. This, though, is only the minimum – there is no upper limit. Every Muslim, however, must provide for his own family first. The amount left over is additional wealth and the amount of zakah which Allah demands is based on this.

TAKE TIME TO THINK

Apart from widows and orphans, can you think of other groups of people that Muslims might feel particularly obliged to help?

OVER TO YOU ▶▶▶

1 Read these quotations from the Hadith:

A "You cannot be a true believer until you wish for your brother what you wish for yourself."

B "One who manages the affairs of the widow and the needy is like one who exerts himself hard in the way of God."

Explain, in your own words, what you think each of these two ahadith are saying.

2 This extract is from the Qur'an:

C "Attend to your prayers and render the alms levy [pay zakat]. Whatever good you do shall be rewarded by God. God is watching all your actions."

Qur'an. Surah 2.110

a) Give one reason why praying and giving to the poor should be linked together.

b) What do you think the Qur'an means when it says: "Whatever good you shall do shall be rewarded by God"?

ZAKAH IS A BLESSING

Zakah is not intended to take away the money and wealth of people. Like other spiritual duties, paying zakah is a blessing to all Muslims.

Paying zakah is an obligation but the Qur'an also recommends the voluntary giving of time, skills and knowledge to help those in need. This is because the poor should be helped towards self-reliance.

Paying zakah is a test of honesty – a Muslim cannot live happily with himself if he does not pay exactly what he owes. He knows that he will have to answer to Allah on the Day of Judgement. The Qur'an tells him that an exact record of all his deeds is being kept in heaven. That record will show if he has been generous and honest.

SADAQAH

Apart from zakah, there is another form of giving for Muslims called sadaqah.

CHECK IT OUT

What is sadaqah?

While zakah is compulsory, sadaqah is optional.

Sadaqah is an act of charity.

Sadaqah may be given at the opening of a new mosque, school or hospital.

Sadaqah can be given at any time.

Sadaqah is often given to thank Allah for success in business, a wedding anniversary, etc.

Sadaqah is a way of thanking Allah and helping the poor at the same time.

You will find out

- The work of Islamic Relief Worldwide.
- The four areas in which the charity works.
- Some of the charity's projects.

In the glossary

Muhammad

Prophet

Qur'an

Islamic Relief Worldwide is committed to making a difference in the lives of children like this.

Wars, floods, earthquakes, drought and famine kill millions of people each year. Those who survive often lose their homes and are forced to live for years in temporary housing without clean water or adequate toilets.

Some of these people remain in refugee camps for years, enduring terrible conditions and running severe health risks. Over 35 million people throughout the world live as refugees.

A *"Islamic Relief seeks to alleviate the suffering, hunger, illiteracy and disease worldwide without regard to colour, race or creed and to provide aid in a compassionate and dignified manner."*

Islamic Relief Worldwide

OVER TO YOU ▶▶▶

1. Explain in one or two sentences the reasons for the existence of the charity Islamic Relief Worldwide.
2. Discuss with your partner what you think Extracts B and C mean and then write your explanations down in your book.
3. Explain the five areas in which Islamic Relief Worldwide works. Add your own comment on why you think each of them is very important.
4. Imagine that you are working for Islamic Relief Worldwide. You are having a discussion with fellow workers about the importance of providing education for girls as well as boys. What arguments would you put forward?

ISLAMIC RELIEF WORLWIDE

Islamic Relief Worldwide was set up in 1984 as a response to the famines that were affecting Africa at the time. You can find the aims of the organisation in Extract A. Islamic Relief Worldwide works in response to this text from the Qur'an:

B *"Whoever saved a life it would be as if he saved the life of all mankind."*

Islamic Relief Worldwide

Islamic Relief Worldwide mainly works in five areas:

*   To provide both short-term aid [Emergency Relief] and long-term aid [Development Projects]. It has emergency teams ready to respond to disasters as soon as they occur.
*   To improve the lives of women and children. These are the two most vulnerable groups in poor countries. In Africa and Asia, for instance, women walk 6km on average each day simply to fetch water for the family.
*   To improve the health of the people. Around 80% of all diseases in the world are due to poor sanitation and inadequate water supplies. Water-borne diseases account for 2.5 million deaths a year – and most of those who die are under the age of five.
*   To fight poverty. Poor living conditions reduce a person's ability to earn a living and reduce the number of children enrolled in school – especially girls. Water shortages lead to poor harvests and hunger. They are all part of the cycle of poverty in poor countries.
*   To provide education. Education is the way out of the poverty trap for millions of people. Even when it is available, education often has very poor resources – open-air schools, poor buildings, few books and teachers, little training. Islamic Relief Worldwide believes that the only way out of poverty is to raise the level of literacy – especially for girls [C].

C *"Educate a boy and you educate one person. Educate a girl and you educate a nation."*

A.Ibn Badis, Algerian Muslim Reform

Islamic Relief Worldwide works throughout the world:

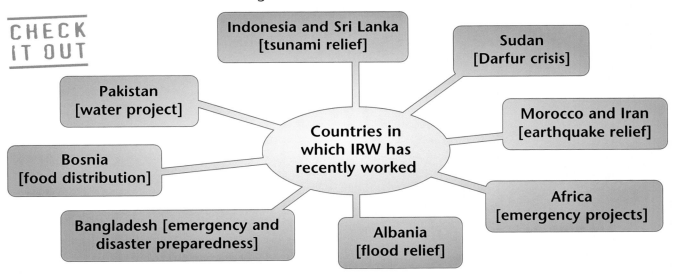

CHECK IT OUT

Indonesia and Sri Lanka [tsunami relief]

Sudan [Darfur crisis]

Pakistan [water project]

Morocco and Iran [earthquake relief]

Bosnia [food distribution]

Countries in which IRW has recently worked

Africa [emergency projects]

Bangladesh [emergency and disaster preparedness]

Albania [flood relief]

CARING FOR ORPHANS

Islamic Relief Worldwide also has an Orphans Welfare Programme which provides care for orphans and other members of their families. This reflects the concern of the Prophet Muhammad for orphans, since he lost his mother and father at a very young age. This programme includes the provision of healthcare and education within their communities.

UNIT 29
CREATION AND PARADISE

You will find out

- The work of Allah in creating the world.

- The importance of human beings.

- About the creation of Adam and Eve and their disobedience.

In the glossary

Allah

Heaven

Iblis

Qur'an

There are close similarities between the way that the Muslim, Jewish and Christian scriptures describe the creation of the world. In particular:

- God creating the world in six days [A].

- The first man and woman being placed in the garden of paradise.

- The first man and woman disobeying God and being banished from the garden.

A *"Your Guardian-Lord is Allah who created the heavens and the earth in six days. He established Himself on the throne [of authority]; He draweth the night as a veil o'er the day, each seeking the other in rapid succession. He created the sun, the moon and the stars, [all] governed by laws under His command. Is it not His to create and to govern? Blessed be Allah, the Cherisher and Sustainer of the Worlds!"*

Qur'an. Surah 7.54

ALLAH CREATED THE WORLD

Muslims believe that Allah created the world and everything in it.

CHECK IT OUT

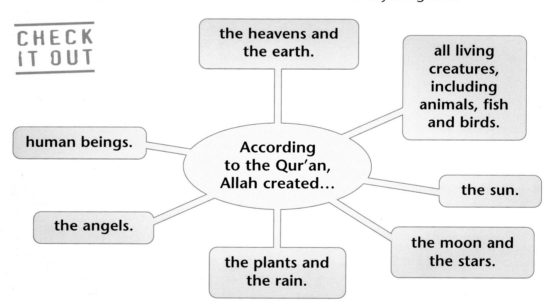

According to the Qur'an, Allah created...
- the heavens and the earth.
- all living creatures, including animals, fish and birds.
- the sun.
- the moon and the stars.
- the plants and the rain.
- the angels.
- human beings.

ON THE DAY OF JUDGEMENT

On the Day of Judgement, everybody will be questioned by Allah on the way that they have taken care of His creation. Those who have polluted or misused Allah's great gifts will not be allowed into heaven. Muslims must be involved in looking after the earth or Allah will judge them very harshly.

SIN IN PARADISE

In creating the world, Allah was assisted by His angels. As His last work of creation, Allah made the first man and woman:

- Allah sent the angels to bring seven handfuls of earth of different colours. From them he made the first man – Adam.
- From Adam's side, Allah made the first woman – Eve.

Adam and Eve were placed in Paradise, a beautiful garden that provided everything that Adam and Eve could possibly need. Only one restriction was placed on the couple. They were not allowed to eat the fruit of the tree of the knowledge of good and evil. Adam and Eve could not resist, however, the voice of the tempter, **Iblis**. He persuaded them to disobey Allah.

WHO WAS IBLIS?

Iblis was the wicked angel who persuaded Adam and Eve to disobey Allah. He was the angel who disobeyed Allah's order that all the angels should bow down and worship the first man, Adam. For his disobedience, Iblis became the tempter who received Allah's permission to test the faith of all Muslim believers.

OVER TO **YOU** ▶▶▶

1. List three common elements between the Muslim, Jewish and Christian stories of creation.
2. Send a letter from a Muslim child to a non-Muslim friend outlining what it is that Muslims believe about creation.
3. Write down all that you know about Iblis.

Muslims believe that human beings have been appointed by Allah to look after the earth. Most religions believe this.

STEWARDS OF CREATION

You will find out

- What Allah expects from human beings in their treatment of the earth.

- The Muslim belief that all parts of creation depend on each other.

- The example that Muhammad sets Muslims in how they should treat creation.

In the glossary

Allah

Hadith

Khalifah

Muhammad

Prophet

Qur'an

Ummah

CHECK IT OUT

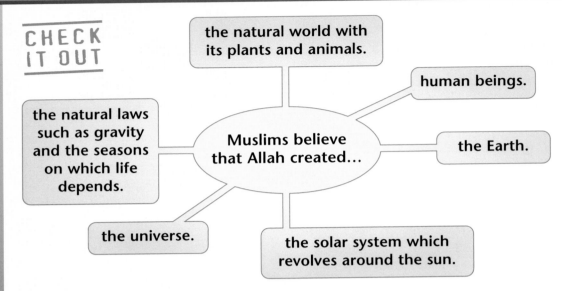

the natural world with its plants and animals.

human beings.

the natural laws such as gravity and the seasons on which life depends.

Muslims believe that Allah created...

the Earth.

the universe.

the solar system which revolves around the sun.

HUMAN BEINGS AND CREATION

Muslims believe that Allah created the world and everything in it. He also created everything that lies beyond it in the universe. As great as these things are, however, human beings are the most important parts of Allah's creation. This is because they alone are able to offer worship to Allah.

A *"It is He who has made You [His] agents, inheritors of the earth."*

Qur'an. Surah 21.107

What does this mean?

- Allah expects human beings to look after the whole of creation. They are called 'stewards' or khalifahs. This simply means that they are caretakers for Allah.
- The Muslim community worldwide, the Ummah, carries the greatest responsibility because it has received Allah's revelation in the Qur'an.
- All human beings will be called to account for the way they have treated Allah's world.
- As the whole of creation was created in a perfect condition so Allah expects it to be returned to him at the end of time in the same condition.

B *"Therefore set your face in worship to the true faith, the original pure state with which God endowed man. God's creation cannot be changed."*

Qur'an. Surah 30.30

Allah created the minutely small.

Allah created the very large.

THE WHOLE OF CREATION HANGS TOGETHER

The Qur'an teaches that the whole of Allah's creation is a unity. Each part of creation depends on every other part and the whole is perfectly balanced. If the health of one part is damaged then the health of the whole is affected.

It is the responsibility of every single human being to look after Allah's creation. Only then can the future health of human beings be guaranteed. Muhammad taught his followers that it is an act of love by human beings to look after creation – for the benefit of all life [C].

C *"If a Muslim plants a tree or sows a field and humans and beasts eat from it all then it is love on his part."*

Muhammad

THE EXAMPLE OF MUHAMMAD

Muhammad is the most important example for Muslims to follow in their everyday lives. He showed his followers the care that is due to all living creatures. They must realise that all animals and insects are part of Allah's creation – no matter how big or small they are.

There are many examples in the Hadith of how the Prophet Muhammad avoided waste, was kind to animals and respected the earth. This is the example that all Muslims must follow.

OVER TO **YOU** ▶▶▶

1 a) What does it mean to call human beings 'stewards' of Allah's creation?
   b) Another word for steward is 'caretaker'. Think of two things that a caretaker is expected to do.
2 Think of three things that show that:
   a) Human beings are good stewards of the earth.
   b) Human beings are bad stewards of the earth.

THE MUSLIM ATTITUDE TO ANIMALS

You will find out

- The Muslim attitude to animals.
- The Muslim attitude to vivisection.
- The use of animal sacrifice in the Muslim festival of Eid-ul-Adha.

In the glossary

Allah

Eid-ul-Adha

Five Pillars

Hajj

Heaven

Ihram

Makkah

Muhammad

Prophet

MUSLIMS AND ANIMALS

Concerning animals and the way they should be treated, the Prophet Muhammad said:

A *"A good deed done to a beast is as good as doing good to a human being: while an act of cruelty to a beast is as good as an act of cruelty to a human being!"*

Hadith

Muslims believe that all animals have been created by Allah and they should be treated with all respect and care. Muslims are allowed to hunt animals but only for food and not for sport. If someone has killed an animal unnecessarily then that animal will testify to Allah against the person on the Day of Judgement. The guilty person will be refused entry into heaven.

Killing for 'a just cause' is the only test whether a human being is justified in killing an animal. Human beings do have dominion over animals but this does not mean that they can do as they please with them. In one of his many sayings, Muhammad commented that:

B *"Whoever kills anything bigger than a sparrow without a just cause, Allah will hold him accountable for it."*

Hadith

EXPERIMENTS ON ANIMALS [VIVISECTION]

In the UK, about three million scientific and medical experiments are carried out on animals – usually rodents – in laboratories each year. These experiments are highly controversial and many people believe that they are unnecessary as it would be possible to use computer simulations to achieve the same results. Other people, however, believe that they are necessary in the fight against disease.

Most Muslims believe that such experiments should be allowed as long as:

- They are important as part of the battle against disease. Muslims believe that human beings, and their welfare, are much more important than the life of an animal.
- The suffering of the animal is no greater than is strictly necessary.
- Animal experiments for cosmetic purposes, or any other trivial reason, are strictly forbidden.

OVER TO YOU ▶▶▶

1 Describe your own feelings about:
   a) The use of animals in experiments to develop better cosmetics.
   b) The use of animals in experiments to find cures for different diseases.

2 Create your own spider diagram to show the Muslim attitude towards animals. Using a different colour pen, add your own views to the diagram.

Slaughtering animals for religious festivals is a feature of more than one religion.

Ihram

Ihram is the practice of undertaking a Hajj [pilgrimage to Makkah], which is one of the Five Pillars of Islam – see unit 9. It is so important that every healthy Muslim is expected to undertake this holy journey once during their lifetime.

The pilgrimage ends with the celebration of the festival of **Eid-ul-Adha**, at which animals are slaughtered and their meat distributed to friends, relations and strangers. Two rules are laid down about the slaughtering of the animals:

- The animals must not be slaughtered in front of other animals.
- A person must not slaughter an animal that he or she has bred.

Take Time to Think

At the festival of Eid-ul-Adha, animals are slaughtered. Which two rules are followed for this? Try to work out with your partner the reasons for these two rules.

65

THE JIHAD

You will find out

- About holy war.
- About the Greater and Lesser Jihad.

In the glossary

Allah

Greater Jihad

Jihad

Lesser Jihad

Madinah

Makkah

Muhammad

Prophet

Qur'an

To Muhammad, Islam was a religion of peace and goodwill. While they lived in Makkah, his followers refused to fight against their enemies. However, in Madinah, Muhammad began to teach that peace and goodwill have to go alongside courage, obedience and duty. **Jihad** means striving against evil and justice for the sake of Allah – wherever it is found.

> **A** "*Permission is given to those who have been attacked unjustly to fight back, God has power to give them victory.*"
>
> Quran. Surah 22.38

A HOLY WAR

Islam, then, is concerned to fight evil in the name of Allah. To do this, the Qur'an teaches that it might be necessary sometimes to go to war. At the same time it lays down the conditions on which a 'holy war' can be fought – and have Allah's support. This could only happen if:

CHECK IT OUT

A 'holy war' can be declared if those fighting...

- are trying to restore peace so that Allah can be freely worshipped.
- are defending the cause of Allah – fighting to gain more land or to conquer others is not allowed.
- as little damage as possible is done to homes and crops.
- every attempt is made to protect civilians from coming to harm.
- women, children, the elderly and the sick receive special protection.
- are under the control of a spiritual and not a military leader.

In the past, and today, Muslims have been accused of spreading their message through force and violence. Some terrorist groups have claimed that this is in keeping with the teaching of the Qur'an. The same charge, of course, has been levelled against other religions in the past. The vast majority of Muslims believe that to do so would be against the teachings of the Qur'an.

All of these Muslims are involved in the Greater Jihad.

FIGHTING INJUSTICE

The jihad is not simply a military war. It is also a moral and spiritual battle. It aims to defeat those people who would hurt and abuse others. It is a struggle to bring freedom and peace to those in need. It looks for every opportunity to spread peace. It accepts the teaching of the Qur'an that:

B *"Good deeds and evil deeds are not equal. Requite [repay] evil with good, and he who is your enemy will become your dearest friend."*

Qur'an. Surah. 41.34

The battle fought against a physical enemy in the name of Allah is known as the **Lesser Jihad**. This is the easier enemy to fight. The enemy within, however, is a far more difficult enemy to defeat. The Prophet Muhammad was returning home from a battle and told his followers that they were now turning from the Lesser Jihad to fight the **Greater Jihad**. All of life from beginning to end is involved in fighting the Greater Jihad. It is in this inner battle that the soul is gradually purified. This is the battle to which the Qur'an refers in this passage:

C *"On the day when every soul will be confronted with all the good it has done, and all the evil it has done, it will wish it were a great distance between it and its evil."*

Qur'an. Surah 3.30

THEY HAVE SAID THAT...

Here are two comments by young Muslims:

To me the jihad is two things. It is a personal struggle in my own life against the sin to which I am prone and all the injustice that I see around me. In the past it was also a physical struggle carried out by Muslims to establish our freedom to worship Allah.

Inshad

The Qur'an teaches Muslims that they have a duty to encourage good and discourage evil. The Prophet said the Lesser Jihad is to fight one's enemies but the Greater one is to confront one's own evil desires.

Youssef

OVER TO YOU ▶▶▶

Look at the two comments by young Muslims:

1 What do you think the sins are that everyone is prone to in their own lives?

2 Why do you think it was so important for Muslims to struggle in the past to achieve freedom of worship?

3 Why do you think that Muhammad suggested that the most important thing was to confront one's own evil desires?

You will find out

- The signs of Allah in the universe.

- About Islam and the origin of the universe.

- About Islam and the theory of evolution.

In the glossary

Allah

Evolution

Big Bang

Qur'an

It is scenes like this that remind Muslims of the existence of Allah.

Islam teaches that there should be no conflict between religion and science. For centuries Islam has taught that Allah has provided science as a way for true believers to find out the truth about the universe and the world in which they live. The Qur'an constantly tells human beings to reflect on and understand this world.

SIGNS OF ALLAH IN THE UNIVERSE

The Qur'an teaches that there are signs of Allah to be found everywhere in the universe if people look with the eyes of faith. They are everywhere:

CHECK IT OUT

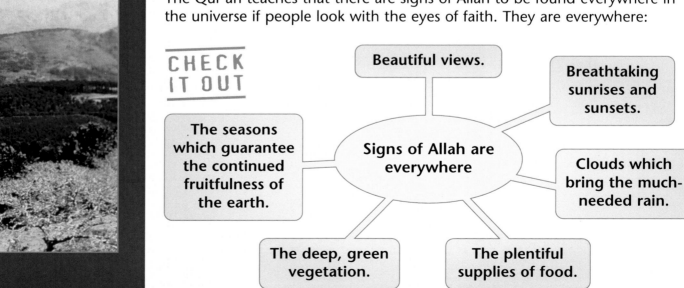

Beautiful views.

Breathtaking sunrises and sunsets.

The seasons which guarantee the continued fruitfulness of the earth.

Signs of Allah are everywhere

Clouds which bring the much-needed rain.

The deep, green vegetation.

The plentiful supplies of food.

In many different places, the Qur'an points out that the wonders of nature draw attention to the power and majesty of Allah. Not everyone, though, is able to see Allah in the world He has made. Such evidence of Allah's existence is only open to those who have the faith to see it [A].

A   *"In the creation of the heavens and the earth and in the alternation of day and night, these are signs for people of understanding."*

Qur'an. Surah 3.191

It asks the simple question, "How could the world have come into being if God had not created it?"

ISLAM AND THE ORIGIN OF THE UNIVERSE

There is a strong similarity between the story of the creation of the universe in the Jewish/Christian scriptures and in the Qur'an. They all teach, for example, that God created the world in six days, out of nothing.

Science talks of the world coming into existence through a **Big Bang**. It does not find any place for God in this event. Islam is happy to accept the idea of a Big Bang at the beginning of everything but believes that Allah brought it about.

Islam is happy to talk of the universe having been created millions of years ago. Like most Jews and Christians, the 'six days' of creation can easily refer to infinitely long periods of time rather than six literal days.

ISLAM AND THE THEORY OF EVOLUTION

Again there are close similarities between the Jewish/Christian stories of the creation of the first human beings and that found in the Qur'an. There would seem to be a conflict between these stories and the theory of **evolution** first suggested by Charles Darwin in the middle of the 19th century.

According to evolution, human beings developed [evolved] from lower forms of life over millions of years. Through a process of 'natural selection', all forms of life either adapted to their changing surroundings – or died out.

None of the creation stories accept this idea happily. All of them suggest that God created all forms of life, and especially human beings, in their final form. All human beings are descended directly from Adam and Eve.

The Qur'an, however, seems to suggest that Allah not only created the perfect world in the first place but also constantly changes it:

B   *"Do they not see how God started the creation and then reproduces it? That is easy enough for God."*

Qur'an. Surah 29.19

This would seem to suggest that there is no great conflict between the teachings of Islam and the theory of evolution.

OVER TO **YOU** ▶▶▶

1 Do you think that:
   a) There is a conflict between Islamic ideas on creation and the Big Bang theory?
   b) Do you think that there is necessarily a conflict between the Muslim story of creation and the theory of evolution?
2 Imagine that you are a young Muslim. Would your faith in Allah be shaken by scientific theories about how the universe, and life, began or not?

GLOSSARY

Abraham [Ibrahim]: The founding father of Judaism and a prophet to Muslims.

Adhan: The call to prayer given by the mu'adhin five times a day.

Allah: The Arabic name for God.

Angel Jibril [Gabriel]: The angel who carried Allah's message to Muhammad.

Aqiqah: The ceremony at which a baby is named.

Big Bang: Scientific theory that the universe began with an enormous explosion.

Bismillah: 'In the name of God.'

Circumcision: The removal of the foreskin of a boy's penis. Also called khitan.

Du'a: Prayers which are said in addition to the salah.

Eid-ul-Adha: A festival which ends the Hajj.

Evolution: Scientific theory that everything evolved [developed] from lesser forms of life.

Extended Family: A family which includes more than two generations living under the same roof or nearby.

Five Pillars: The five basic beliefs of Islam.

Greater Jihad: The battle which every Muslim is called to fight against sin.

Hadith: Collection of sayings and stories from the Prophet Muhammad.

Hajj: The pilgrimage to Makkah, one of the Five Pillars.

Halal: Food, clothing or behaviour which is correct for a Muslim.

Heaven: The place of paradise after death.

Hell: The place of everlasting torment for the wicked in eternity.

Hijab: Clothing worn by many Muslim women.

Iblis: The power opposed to God.

Imam: Man who leads prayers in a mosque.

Ihram: White clothing worn on the Hajj.

Jihad: 'Striving' or 'holy war'.

Ka'bah: The holiest shrine in Islam, in Makkah.

Khalifah: Name given to human beings as caretakers of the world and its resources.

Khitan: See circumcision.

Khutbah: The sermon at Friday Prayers given by the imam.

Lesser Jihad: The physical fighting to defend Islam.

Madinah: The city where Muhammad set up his capital after his migration from Makkah in 622CE.

Madraseh: The school held in a mosque to teach children Arabic and the Qur'an.

Makkah: The holiest city in Islam, where the Prophet Muhammad was born.

Mihrab: The alcove in the mosque wall indicating the direction of Makkah.

Minaret: The tower attached to a mosque from which the call to prayer is given.

Minbar: The raised platform used by the imam to preach at Friday Prayers.

Mosque: The 'place of prostration', the place of prayer for Muslims.

Mu'adhin: The man who calls Muslims to prayer five times a day.

Muhammad: The last and most important of the prophets of Allah.

Prophet: A messenger from Allah.

Qiblah: A wall in the mosque facing Makkah.

Qur'an: The holy book of Islam.

Rak'ah: A sequence of prayers during salah.

Ramadan: The month when Muslims fast.

Sadaqah: Voluntary donations to charity.

Salah: Praying, one of the Five Pillars of Islam.

Sawm: Fasting during the month of Ramadan.

Shahadah: The first, and most important, of the Five Pillars of Islam.

Shari'ah: Laws laid down in the Qur'an.

Shi'ite Muslims: One of the two branches of Islam.

Sunnah: The actions of Muhammad.

Sunni Muslims: One of the two branches of Islam.

Surah: A verse in the Qur'an.

Tasbih: Prayer beads.

Tawhid: The fundamental Muslim belief that there is only one God.

Ulama: The leading Muslims who chose the successor to Muhammad.

Ummah: The worldwide Muslim community.

Wudu: The washing ritual performed by a Muslim prior to prayer.

Zakah: The compulsory payment of 2.5% of your salary to charity, the third of the Five Pillars of Islam.

Badger Publishing Limited
Suite G08, Business & Technology Centre
Bessemer Drive
Stevenage
Hertfordshire
SG1 2DX
Tel: 01438 791037
Fax: 01438 791036

Badger KS3 Religious Education
Muslim Beliefs and Issues

First published 2007
ISBN 978-1-84691-088-3

Text © Michael Keene 2007
Complete work © Badger Publishing Limited 2007

Acknowledgements
Photos © Alex Keene, The Walking Camera, with the following exceptions:
P.11 Prayer beads © Action Press, P.21 Makkah © Sharok Hatami / **Rex Features**.
P.23 Hell (oil on panel) by Bosch, Hieronymus (c.1450-1516) (school of) Hermitage, St. Petersburg, Russia. Dutch, out of copyright from www.bridgeman.co.uk.
P.34 Adhan, P.57 Zakah © Christine Osborne, World Religions Photo Library; P.47 Ramadan © Julia Waterlow, Eye Ubiquitous; P.66 Muslims © Paula Solloway / **Alamy**.
P.36 Couple © Ricki Rosen, CORBIS SABA – **CORBIS**.
P.39 Burial © AFP, P.62 Ants © Gerry Ellis, Digital Vision, P.65 Eid-ul-Adha © Stringer, Getty Images News / **Getty Images**.

Publisher: David Jamieson
Editor: Paul Martin
Designer: Adam Wilmott
Cover photo: Alex Keene